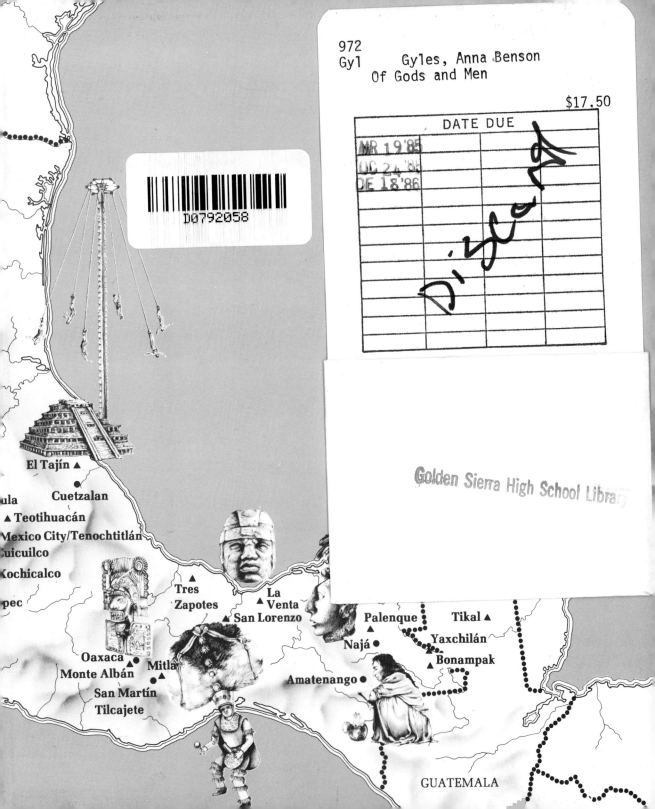

DATE DUE		
MR 19'85		
OC 24'85		
DE 18'86		

El Tajín ▲

Cuetzalan ●

▲ Teotihuacán

Mexico City/Tenochtitlán

Cuicuilco

Xochicalco

Tres Zapotes ▲

La Venta ▲

San Lorenzo ▲

Palenque ▲   Tikal ▲

Najá ●   Yaxchilán

Bonampak ▲

Oaxaca ▲

Monte Albán ●   Mitla ▲

Amatenango ●

San Martín Tilcajete

GUATEMALA

Of Gods and Men

Of Gods and Men

The Heritage of Ancient Mexico

Anna Benson Gyles and Chloë Sayer

HARPER & ROW, PUBLISHERS, New York
Cambridge, Philadelphia, San Francisco,
London, Mexico City, Saõ Paulo, Sydney

1817

FIRST U.S. EDITION

ISBN: 0-06-014887-X

LIBRARY OF CONGRESS CATALOG CARD NUMBER: 81-47229

81 82 83 84 10 9 8 7 6 5 4 3 2 1

Contents

Acknowledgements   5

Introduction   9

1 The First Temples   29

2 The Empire Builders   56

3 The People of the Valley   87

4 The People of the Rainforest   120

5 The Survivors:

The Christian Compromise   171

6 The Survivors:

The Way of the Ancestors   195

Picture Acknowledgements   221

Bibliography   222

Index   229

For this U.S. edition, colour plates (following pages 64 and 128) are reproduced in black and white.

Acknowledgements

In this book we have tried to give a flavour of the extraordinary civilisations that made up pre-Hispanic Mexico and to show how many of its ancient customs and beliefs have survived among the Indians today. In no way can it be considered anything more than an introduction to this vast and complex subject.

The book is based on a series of films made for BBC Television. We spent over three months filming in Mexico and were guided throughout by our two eminent advisors Miss Elizabeth Carmichael of the British Museum (who also copiously advised on the text of this book) and the late Dr Alberto Ruz of the Museum of Anthropology in Mexico City. We were also fortunate in being able to work very closely with his son, Jorge Ruz, who very kindly introduced us to the legendary Gertrude Duby-Blom. Through her good offices we were able to visit the Lacandón Indians, a people with whom she has lived and worked for over forty years. We should also like to thank the Instituto Nacional de Antropología e Historia and the Instituto Nacional Indigenista for their co-operation, and in London we are particularly indebted to the Cultural Attaché at the Mexican Embassy, Sr Horacio Flores-Sanchez, for all his help and encouragement with our project.

All through our visit to Mexico we had the invaluable assistance of Marcos Ortiz. He miraculously organised expeditions to the most remote parts of the country and through his personal friendship with the Indian people we were able to film unique festivals and ceremonies. But perhaps the major burden of our project fell onto the shoulders of our production team. They put up with sleepless nights in cowsheds, nights spent swinging in hammocks or creeping round museums, with endless early-morning calls, broken-down cars and bumpy aeroplane trips. Throughout all our adventures we were supported and encouraged by a most talented and enthusiastic group of people: cameramen John Hooper and Colin Waldeck; sound recordists Alan Cooper and Bob Roberts; assistant cameramen John Adderley and David Bennett. Keeping us all together and in high spirits were our two production assistants,

Rosalind Bentley and Alexandra Branson. Tucked away in a tiny cutting room in London, away from the glamour of the foreign location, our film editor Raoul Sobel spent almost a year trying to make sense of all our efforts, bringing to the project his extraordinary skill and judgement. Now, thanks to the guidance and enthusiasm of Stephen Davies of BBC Publications, the series has been turned into a book.

But above all we owe our thanks to the Indians of Mexico, who allowed us into their homes, who welcomed us to their private ceremonies and who overwhelmed us with their friendship and hospitality.

Anna Benson Gyles
Chloë Sayer
1980

Of Gods and Men

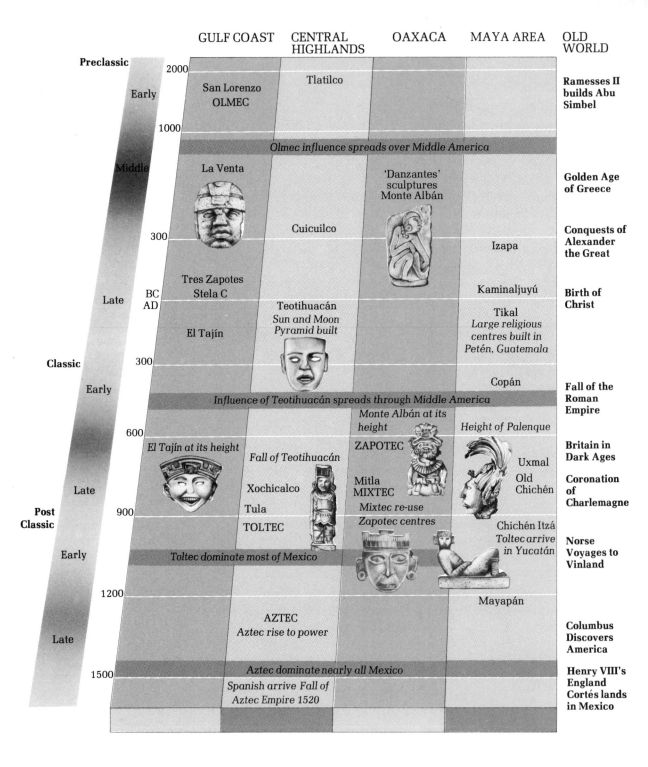

	GULF COAST	CENTRAL HIGHLANDS	OAXACA	MAYA AREA	OLD WORLD
Preclassic — Early	2000 — San Lorenzo OLMEC	Tlatilco			Ramesses II builds Abu Simbel
	1000				
	Olmec influence spreads over Middle America				
Middle	La Venta		'Danzantes' sculptures Monte Albán		Golden Age of Greece
	300	Cuicuilco		Izapa	Conquests of Alexander the Great
Late	Tres Zapotes Stela C			Kaminaljuyú	Birth of Christ
	BC AD	Teotihuacán *Sun and Moon Pyramid built*		Tikal *Large religious centres built in Petén, Guatemala*	
	El Tajín				
Classic — Early	300			Copán	Fall of the Roman Empire
	Influence of Teotihuacán spreads through Middle America				
	600		Monte Albán at its height	Height of Palenque	Britain in Dark Ages
	El Tajín at its height	*Fall of Teotihuacán*	ZAPOTEC	Uxmal	Coronation of Charlemagne
Late		Xochicalco	Mitla MIXTEC	Old Chichén	
	900	Tula	*Mixtec re-use Zapotec centres*	Chichén Itzá *Toltec arrive in Yucatán*	Norse Voyages to Vinland
Post Classic — Early	TOLTEC				
	Toltec dominate most of Mexico				
	1200			Mayapán	
Late		AZTEC *Aztec rise to power*			Columbus Discovers America
	1500	*Aztec dominate nearly all Mexico*			Henry VIII's England Cortés lands in Mexico
		Spanish arrive Fall of Aztec Empire 1520			

Introduction

Few countries in the world have such extreme variations of landscape and climate as Mexico: hot steamy rainforests on the coast, bleak, hostile deserts in the north, huge mountain ranges and snow-peaked volcanoes, the flat limestone peninsula of Yucatán. Land so fertile that crops can be sown and harvested three times a year, and land so arid that nothing but cactus will grow. These contrasts have shaped man's life in Mexico. No region has ever been self-sufficient. From the earliest times separate areas have always depended on one another, exchanging produce and ideas. This is why, despite differences of language and culture, it was possible for great changes and new advances to be felt rapidly throughout the country. Nothing has had such a profound effect on the civilisations of Mexico as this constant interchange of culture and ideas.

Mexico is shaped rather like a funnel, covering an area of 761,830 square miles, and is the third largest country in Latin America. It is bordered on the north by the United States of America, and on the south by Guatemala and Belize. To the west is the Pacific ocean, and to the east lie the Gulf of Mexico and the Caribbean Sea. The central land mass is an uneven plateau flanked by an eastern and western range of mountains called the Sierra Madre, which run roughly parallel to the coast. The northern part of Mexico is arid and thinly-populated. The mountainous southern end of the plateau is the heart of Mexico, where over half the population live.

Much of Mexico sits precariously above a volcanic belt that periodically rocks the country with tremors and earthquakes. It is one of the most active volcanic zones in the world. Near the centre of this belt, high up in a small basin, lies Mexico City. Seismologists think that it would have disappeared long ago were it not cushioned from the worst of the violence by the subterranean sea of mud on which it rests.

With a rapidly growing population that already exceeds 13,000,000, Mexico's capital is a metropolis teeming with activity. Politics, commerce, industry and culture are all centred in this gigantic city where ultra-modern skyscrapers, office blocks and factories tower above Colonial-style buildings, tree-lined avenues, parks and open-air markets. A ceaseless flow of traffic roars along the main roads, passing huge supermarkets, elegant department stores and makeshift stalls on street corners that sell food and flowers.

Mexico City now houses one in six Mexicans, and other towns are also expanding fast, but over half the population still lives in the country and works the land. Despite Mexico's vast size, less than 15 per cent of the land is suitable for farming, and huge commercially-run holdings alternate with small, overcrowded tracts of land cultivated along traditional lines. The crops, like the farming methods, vary considerably. Maize, sometimes known as sweetcorn, remains the basic crop and the

Planting maize with traditional digging sticks

staple of the Mexican diet, but black beans, squash, tomatoes, cacao, avocado and innumerable varieties of chili peppers are among the many indigenous foods that are still widely grown. Wheat and other crops introduced from the Old World have also become an integral part of farming, and the raising of cattle and poultry has come to play an important role in the national economy.

Yet despite an impressive agricultural record, it is proving increasingly hard to keep pace with the Mexican birth rate. The population, which now stands at 69,000,000, is likely to have doubled by the year 2000, and unemployment is already a chronic problem. Recent governments have done their best to promote industry, and over the past few decades Mexico has gone from a simple economy based on farming and handicrafts to one that boasts new mills for making steel, cellulose, paper, coke and cement. There are factories for producing all kinds of appliances and electrical equipment, and processing plants for chemicals, pharmaceuticals, fertilisers and food. Then in 1979 the world's press gave headline space to Mexico: the oil boom had arrived.

Oil is not a new source of wealth in Mexico. Considerable international ill-feeling was stirred up in 1938 when President Cárdenas expropriated the oil companies which were then largely in the hands of foreign entrepreneurs. Pemex, the Mexican state petroleum monopoly, was founded to take control of the oil which was known to exist in large quantities, and it became Mexico's biggest single source of revenue. In 1976, however, the current president, José Lopez Portillo, took office and he directed the oil company to step up exploration in the south-east of Mexico. The gamble paid off handsomely, and since then Pemex has been drilling an average of 75 new wells a month under the Bay of Campeche and in the states of Chiapas and Tabasco, where gigantic pipelines, cooling towers and rigs rise up out of the once green and lush forests. By early 1980, Mexico was exporting over 1,000,000 barrels of oil to the US each day, and this figure is expected to rise still higher.

Oil, which has become the most sought-after commodity in the modern world, is often known as 'black gold'. But it was real gold that first lured foreigners to these shores. In the sixteenth century Europe was obsessed with the quest for that valuable substance which, alone among metals, neither tarnished nor decayed. To the Europeans it seemed the most perfect and precious of materials—the symbol of eternal life. Men took to the seas in search of exotic lands where they might find the legendary El Dorado—the Golden One.

In 1519 a Spanish expedition reached Mexico, and here at last they found gold in abundance. But Hernán Cortés and his soldiers also found advanced civilisations, with complex traditions and beliefs. Peoples who had developed a form of writing, sophisticated calendar systems and a vigesimal (by twenties) method of counting. Peoples who were architects, poets, craftsmen and statesmen. The Mexican Indian was essentially a religious person, and it was his religion that inspired his art, architecture and way of life. The Spanish *Conquistadores* took little interest in the beliefs of others. Their hunger for gold was matched by their zeal for winning converts to Catholicism. Within a few years of their arrival, they had

Spanish church built on the ruins of the ancient Mixtec temple at Mitla in Oaxaca

stripped the country of its treasures, smashed its civilisation and reduced its people to the level of slaves, forcing the Mexican Indian to adopt the 'true faith'.

The Church sanctioned the Conquest for the sake of gaining souls, yet it took a long time deciding whether the Indians actually had the same sort of souls as Europeans. The Indian cause was energetically upheld by Bartolomé de las Casas, Bishop of the Maya province of Chiapas, who carried his campaign to Spain, complaining that Indians were being treated as 'of less worth than bedbugs'. In the meantime the orders of the Franciscans, Dominicans, Augustinians, and later on the Jesuits, debated the best way to defeat idolatry and paganism. On the ruins of Indian temples, churches were erected, and mass Catholic rites were held so that Indians could be baptised by the thousand. But the planting of Christianity in Mexico took more than impressive religious ceremonies and the dedicated preaching of monks. It took a miracle.

In 1531, exactly ten years after the Aztec empire had been crushed, the Spanish were able to report that the Virgin Mary had appeared to a newly-baptised Indian. She ordered the building of a church in her name, and gave the Indian proof of her miraculous powers by imprinting her likeness on his cloak. She appeared draped in a long mantle of blue patterned with stars, and wearing a white robe embroidered with gold designs. But one factor was to prove especially significant: she was dark-skinned. At last the Indians had a saint of their own with whom they could identify. A papal bull later declared the Virgin of Guadalupe, as she became known, the patroness and protectoress of Mexico.

Between the Spanish Conquest and the Revolution of 1910, a period of nearly 400 years, the condition of the Indian peasant was one of great and growing misery. Spanish grandees had taken over the estates that once belonged to the Indian lords. Spanish viceroys implemented the harsh laws of Colonial rule. Wealthy, high-born Spaniards held all government posts. Everyone else was excluded, even Spaniards who had been born in Mexico, and who were pejoratively labelled as 'creoles'. Nearly all the fertile land was owned by absentee Spanish landlords or by the Roman Catholic Church, and the Indian peasant was often little more than a semi-enslaved *peon* working on the great *haciendas* of the rich. His standard of living was deplorable, and he was allowed to own little or no land. There was also the threat of the mines: the sources of silver and gold had soon been located, and vast numbers of Indians were uprooted and put to work as virtual slaves.

Under Colonial rule a new class began to emerge however. It was made up of *mestizos*, the offspring of Indian and Spanish parents. By the beginning of the nineteenth century this class alone far outnumbered the pure-blooded Spaniards, whose domination was bitterly resented by *mestizos*, creoles and Indians alike. In 1810 the standard of revolt was raised by a priest, Father Miguel Hidalgo y Costillo. With his slogan 'Long Live Our Lady of Guadalupe, Perish the Spaniards', he collected over 80,000 supporters. Eleven years later in 1821, independence was finally won. But during the long struggle against the Spanish government, bitter differences had broken out within the revolutionary group. The '1821 Independence' was followed by a series of wars and uprisings led by the many separate political groups which had emerged. It was not until 1857 that a period of reform began.

In that year Benito Juárez, a Zapotec Indian, was elected President and he embarked on a liberal programme of education, freedom of the press and above all the separation of Church and State. But the Church, in league with the wealthy Spanish landowners, opposed the new régime and civil war broke out. Benito Juárez and his supporters eventually won, but Mexico was financially ruined. The Indian President was forced to suspend payment of the national debt, and a joint force of British, Spaniards and French landed in Mexico to protect their financial rights. The British and the Spaniards soon withdrew, but the French pushed inland and succeeded in 1863 in occupying Mexico City. Napoleon III capitalised on this victory by appointing Archduke Maximilian of Austria as the emperor of Mexico.

Maximilian's reign was to be extremely short. In 1867, at the insistence of the United States, the French forces withdrew leaving the Archduke to fend for himself. Deserted and betrayed, he was captured by supporters of Benito Juárez and shot. Juárez was again in control of the country, and he resumed his programme of reforms. He died in 1872 from natural causes, and was succeeded by the distinguished scholar Lerdo de Tejada. Within a short time, however, Tejada had been overthrown by Porfirio Díaz. Although Díaz became a ruthless dictator, he did introduce a period of peace and prosperity. Mexican finances were put on a sound basis, industries were built up and international relations improved. But the mass of illiterate and half-starved peasants had never been so wretched. Their lands were stolen, their personal liberties taken away, and many were sold into forced labour on the tobacco plantations. It was this gulf between the dazzling prosperity of the ruling class and the terrible distress of the peasants which led to the uprising of 1910.

Porfirio Díaz was driven into exile and the old system of government was swept away. 'Land and Liberty' became the new cry, but for several years the situation in Mexico verged on chaos. Revolutionaries such as Pancho Villa, Emiliano Zapata and Álvaro Obregón became legends in their own lifetimes. Then in 1917 a new constitution was drafted which is still in force today, and in 1929 the Partido Revolucionario Institucional was formed. Today the Revolutionary party, or the PRI as it is known for short, is still in power. Each president is elected for a term of six years, and he appoints his team of government ministers. The PRI continues to see itself as the party of the people, incorporating the social-democratic ideals of the revolution. But despite their efforts they have still not succeeded in bridging the gap between rich and poor.

Although much has been done to redistribute the land, and to give the peasant either communal or personal control over the land he cultivates, rates of income remain low. His

Fetching water in Zoatecpan—one of the many villages where the Aztec language of Nahuatl is still spoken (*see also colour plates 7 and 8*)

minimum wage barely allows him a simple diet of beans, rice and tortillas. His wife may have the vote, his children may sometimes go to school, and his family may receive some help from the state, but his house is often just a shack of mud-brick and thatch with earthen floors, no windows, no running water and no sanitation.

The ruggedness of the landscape has made modernisation difficult in many parts of the country. But the forests, deserts and mountain ranges of Mexico have also helped to shelter large pockets of Indians, enabling them to preserve many of their old customs and traditions. Although some groups have not survived to modern times, there are still nearly sixty different peoples, giving Mexico a total pure-blooded Indian population of more than seventeen million.

Some have had very little contact with the outside world. To protect themselves from Spanish domination, they retreated deeper into their inhospitable surroundings and were allowed to remain there because their land was uninviting, and because they had nothing on it to attract outsiders. Other Indians were less fortunate, however, because a more open environment made them vulnerable. Loss of lands, compulsory resettlement and forced labour were some of the consequences. But despite outside influence, these groups have also clung to their Indian identity.

Language is one of the most important of the many bonds which unite members of a group. Almost all the different Indian peoples of Mexico have kept their ancient languages, which are often mutually unintelligible, and in remote areas there are whole villages where Spanish is neither spoken nor understood. Costume acts as another bond. In ancient Mexico, costume differences showed the wearer's cultural and geographical origins and many Indian communities have adhered to a particular style of dress, with variations to distinguish each village within that community.

The Conquest saw the overthrow of the priests and rulers who had formed the élite of the great Indian civilisations. What remained was a peasant class dependent for survival on hunting and fishing, but mostly on agriculture. In remote areas farming methods and crops have sometimes changed surprisingly little. The land which belongs to Indians is often difficult to cultivate, with steep slopes and rocky crevices, and traditional tools are still the best suited. Fields are cleared by cutting down and burning the trees and undergrowth, and seeds are sown with the help of a digging stick. In most communities the staple diet consists of beans, squash, chili peppers and above all maize, which is eaten in a variety of ways but most often in the form of the *tortilla* or maize pancake.

Settlement patterns vary from group to group. Some Indians prefer to remain in closely-knit villages with their fields on the perimeter. Other communities are made up of family units scattered in small settlements over vast distances, and some are still semi-nomadic. Natural surroundings provide basic building materials, and traditionally most houses are made from mud-brick, wood or poles, and thatch. Often consisting of just one room, they have floors of stamped earth and no windows. Cooking is sometimes done outside, but if not the roof may have a hole for the smoke to escape. There is little furniture in an Indian household, and during the day most tasks are performed out of doors.

Although the Indian peoples of Mexico are no longer great architects as so many of their ancestors were, they have inherited a number of their skills. Most communities specialise in a particular craft such as potting, basketry, wood-carving or weaving on a waist-strap loom. Some skills have not changed at all in hundreds of years, while others have been enriched by the introduction of new materials and techniques such as the glazing of pottery or the use of the treadle loom for weaving. In remote areas villages often complement one another's material

Houses surrounded by maize fields in the Mixteca mountains of Oaxaca

needs. While one might keep the region supplied with hand-coiled pots, another provides woven cloth or palm hats. In this way many Indian communities have been able to remain self-supporting, producing their own food and supplementing their income by trading locally at markets and fairs.

Although a few Indian groups have kept to their ancient religions, most were, nominally at least, converted to Christianity soon after the Conquest. Spanish monks, often travelling long distances on foot, succeeded in taking the teachings of the Roman Catholic Church into deep forests, mountain fastnesses and deserts. One need only look at most Mexican landscapes to appreciate the tremendous impact they had. At the heart of innumerable villages, no matter how small or how remote, stands a Colonial church built with Indian labour. The friars who directed them gave each community a patron saint, and taught them to celebrate the Christian festivals, many of which had similarities with indigenous rites. The Indian was naturally attracted to the Catholic religion with its pomp and ceremony, its highly decorated altars ablaze with candles and its richly-garbed priests. Many villages are now without resident priests, but the traditions instilled by the early friars are kept alive by the Indians themselves, who have often fused the Christian teachings with their own ancient beliefs.

In all Catholic communities the saints are greatly loved and respected. Their images take pride of place in the churches where they are brought offerings of food, flowers and incense. On feast days they are paraded through the village and dressed in splendour. But it is quite common among Indian groups to find that the saints have been identified with the old gods. Among the descendants of the Aztec the Virgin Mary has assumed the attributes of Tonantzin, an Earth Goddess, and she is sometimes even called by that name as a sign of affection. Some Maya peoples associate St Thomas with rain, and in one community whenever rain is needed the saint is brought out of the church and left to stand in the heat of the midday sun 'so that he can feel what his people are feeling'. Sometimes Bible lore has been adapted to suit the Indian view of the world, or to make it more personal, and villagers frequently explain that St John or even Jesus Christ actually visited their region. Religious belief is also linked with the natural habitat where local hills or springs may be thought of as holy, and even the cross—the symbol of Christianity—has an ancient significance. In use long before the arrival of the Spaniards, the cross is still linked by many Indian groups with rain, the growth of maize and with the four cardinal points, as well as with the Tree of Life which has its roots in the Underworld and its branches in the Heavens.

Religious fervour, which runs high throughout the year, finds its chief expression on feast days. In ancient Mexico the calendar was dominated by festivals in honour of the gods, and some of the early friars saw that the task of conversion could be helped by incorporating the Indians' own ceremonial music, dances and songs into the Catholic service while eliminating the more pagan elements. Although new dances evolved, many of the old ones have survived, and today they are performed in honour of the saints in the church atrium or even inside the

Religious procession in the Totonac village of Huehuetla, Puebla

church itself. As in the past the dances are a way of praying, and performers are fulfilling a religious vow on behalf of the whole village.

Although Christianity annihilated the learned priests who once ruled over the destinies of the great civilisations of ancient Mexico, some of their power was inherited by humbler village holy men or shamans. Among the few remaining Indian groups where Catholic teachings have had no influence, shamans control the spiritual life of their followers. And even in ostensibly Christian communities, there are wise men and women who can cure illnesses with herbs, and who treat the sick when orthodox medicine is unpopular or scarce. Some also claim to have magic powers. These enable them to cast or dissolve spells, and to preside over agricultural rituals on behalf of villagers who make offerings to the forces of the earth in return for rain and a good harvest.

Ceremonies, whether purely Christian or with pagan overtones, can demand a large outlay of money, food, possessions and time. Like their ancestors, Indians make few distinctions between the divine and the secular. Families tend to share their resources and to give their labour generously, motivated by the strength of their faith and by their loyalty to the community.

But even the remnants of the old civilisations are gradually being lost, as many Indians move into the big cities or even cross the border into the United States in search of work. The Instituto Nacional Indigenista, or INI as it is called for short, is a government organisation responsible for helping Indians who stay on their land to adopt new farming methods and crops, and to improve their standards of hygiene and housing. The government is also pursuing its policy of education, and many villages now have schools where Spanish is taught. As contact with the outside world increases, many traditions are lost and craft skills forgotten. Plastics and synthetic materials are already replacing clay cooking pots and richly woven textiles, and modern farming implements are overtaking the traditional tools. But even in outlying areas, where Indian culture has survived best, a renewal of missionary zeal, represented by the Wycliffe Bible Translators and the Summer School of Linguistics from the USA, bids fair to wipe out the last traces of pre-Hispanic religion.

But as the past recedes, there is in Mexico and abroad a reawakening of interest in the Indian heritage. Many people in the West, having imposed their own way of life on so much of the rest of humanity, now find their own faiths dying. They look towards alien cultures with renewed interest and respect. Tourists come in their thousands to see the archaeological sites, and to walk round the museums, for Mexico has more vivid reminders of its past than almost any other country in the world. Pyramids, temples and ruined cities rise from the plains or lie almost buried in tropical rainforests. There are over 11,000 known archeological sites, many of them still un-excavated.

Important new discoveries are still being made. As recently

as 1975 some of the best preserved wall-paintings ever found in Mexico were uncovered eighty miles from Mexico City at Cacaxla. Archaeologists received an anonymous telephone call from a rather hysterical man, who told them that he had been looking for loot in an unexcavated mound when the rubble fell away, revealing a hole which led into an inner chamber. He peered through, and there before him were Apache Indians! The archaeologists suspected that this was some kind of hoax, but decided nevertheless to investigate. When they visited the site, they were astounded. The 'Apache Indians' were in fact beautiful wall-paintings dating from about AD 750. They had

Warrior engaged in battle from wall paintings at Cacaxla (*see also colour plate 23*)

been carefully covered over, in antiquity, before the site was abandoned, and showed scenes symbolic of water and fertility. Further excavations revealed other paintings of warriors engaged in battle that date from about AD 600. The whole site is now being excavated, and is providing invaluable information about a crucial period in Mexican history.

As well as excavating new sites, archaeologists are also studying the mass of written material that has survived, in an attempt to piece together the complex history of pre-Conquest civilisations. Many of the peoples of ancient Mexico had a form of writing, although only with the Maya was a hieroglyphic script developed which can truly be called writing in our sense: the simpler use of hieroglyphics in Central Mexico was largely pictographic or ideographic. Their records were painted on deerskin, which was then folded rather like an accordion. These

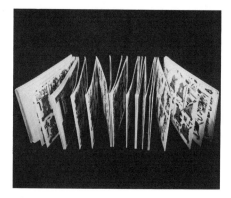

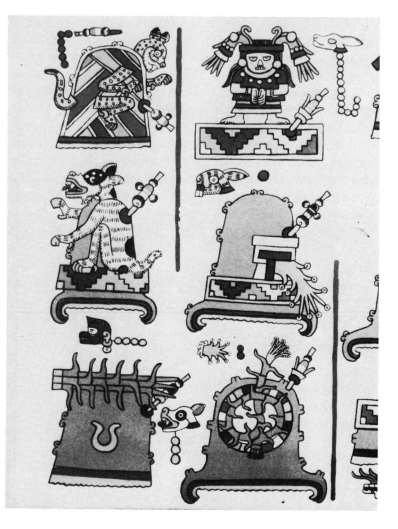

Above Facsimile of the Mixtec codex known as Zouche-Nuttall; *right* Detail from the Zouche-Nuttall codex

'books', which are usually referred to as codices, dealt with such subjects as mythology, ritual, divination and genealogy. Most of them were destroyed by the Spanish missionaries as works of superstition and witchcraft, but from the few that have survived, scholars are beginning to interpret the meaning of many of the painted figures and scenes. As well as these pictorial manuscripts, there are chronicles written by the Spanish conquerors, the soldiers, officials and missionaries.

There are also Indian-language works written in the European alphabet soon after the arrival of the Spaniards. One of the most ambitious ethnographic enterprises of the early Colonial period was undertaken by a friar, Bernardino de

Sahagún. He gathered round him wise and experienced Indians who had survived the Conquest, and between them they compiled a twelve-volume treatise dictated in the Aztec language, Nahuatl, by the Indians themselves. Sahagún called it '*La Historia General de las Cosas de la Nueve España*' or 'The General History of the Things of New Spain'.

Some of these ancient manuscripts are housed in the National Museum of Anthropology in Mexico City, a museum entirely devoted to the arts and culture of the Mexican Indian. The museum is now situated in Chapultepec Park, and is the pride of Mexico. Architecturally and for its methods of presentation the museum is considered to be one of the finest in the world. The formation of the collection began as far back as 1790, when three immense monoliths, including the Aztec Sun Stone, were accidentally discovered in Mexico City. For the first time since the Spanish Conquest, the authorities decided not to destroy pagan idols. They had begun to realise that only through such objects could the forgotten history of their country be reconstructed. The preservation of those three Aztec pieces formed the basis of the museum's now famous collection.

Today the National Museum displays an incredible array of pre-Hispanic artefacts ranging from the early hunting period of 10,000 BC to the fall of the Aztec empire in 1521. In room after room visitors are brought face to face with the peoples of the past : the Olmec from the Gulf Coast who carved the huge stone heads; the Maya, who became the great astronomers and mathematicians of Middle America; the Zapotec and the Mixtec from the Valley of Oaxaca, who were among the most talented craftsmen in Mexico; the warlike Toltec who swept across the Valley of Mexico; and the Aztec who in less than a hundred years developed an immense empire.

The upper storey of the museum is devoted to the Indians of today. Ten large halls show textiles, jewellery, agricultural tools, reconstructed huts and scenes with people going about their daily tasks. But Mexican Indians rarely come to their museum, nor do the poorer inhabitants of Mexico City. They find it a daunting place, full of rules and regulations. The Museum is currently trying to change this attitude with an innovatory scheme that involves taking the museum to the people. The man behind this project is the Museum's Assistant Director, Mario Vázquez. He and his team are committed to taking mobile museums to deprived areas of the city. Although

Aztec stone sculpture showing Xochipilli, god of music, song and love

he believes that the big museums of the world will always have an important role to play, he is more concerned with reaching the sort of public which might normally feel excluded. He explains his views like this:

> If museums don't serve their community, they are in danger of becoming dead institutions. I believe that if a museum is to be useful, then it must be a part of everyday life. This is the idea behind the project which my team and I call 'La Casa del Museo', or 'The House of the Museum'. We want to go out to small communities, to the slum areas of the city where people are often hungry for culture. I mean by that that they are searching for the sort of knowledge that will help them with all the problems they have to face daily.
>
> Of course one could ask why a museum like ours which is concerned with the study of anthropology should be intervening in people's lives like this. But after all, what is anthropology?

Setting up the mobile museum or *Casa del Museo* on the outskirts of Mexico City

> It's the study of man in all his aspects, whether these are linked with archaeology, ethnology, history, nutrition or whatever. And these are the very themes we want to concentrate on in our museums.

The idea for the project came to Mario Vázquez after an exhibition which he had planned for UNESCO on the over-population of cities and the problems of rural migration. He realised that the people who had most to gain from such an

The local community visiting the finished museum

exhibition, and who were most directly concerned, would not be attending, because they were poor and uneducated, and because all their time was taken up just working to survive. It was then that he decided to create a new type of museum, one which could enter the lives of such people. Working with funds allotted to him by the Museum of Anthropology, he set up the first Casa del Museo in 1972 in a shanty town, where the poor from the country had settled in the hope of finding work. At the present time there are two such centres; a third will be opening shortly, and there are plans for many more.

One of the communities to be served by the Casa del Museo is Santo Domingo, where 150,000 people live in an area covering just over three-quarters of a square mile. These are for the most part country people, who have emigrated to the city from all over Mexico. On one single night in December 1974, no less than 30,000 squatters invaded Santo Domingo, eventually building themselves homes. Astounding though this figure seems, it is by no means unique in Mexico City where organised newcomers, faced with unemployment and lack of housing, frequently move into unoccupied stretches of land on the outskirts of the city and build shanty towns almost overnight. Squatters of this type have been colloquially nicknamed '*paracaistas*' or 'parachutists', because of the speed and the unexpected manner of their arrival, and these makeshift towns are known as '*ciudades perdidas*' or 'lost cities'.

Like squatters in other places, the settlers at Santo Domingo had to fight hard at the beginning to get the already over-burdened civic authorities to grant them services and schools. Eventually they succeeded, but unemployment, poverty and overcrowded living conditions are still a fact of life. This is just the sort of urban community that Mario Vázquez and his team are hoping to reach with their project, and their museum has received an enthusiastic welcome. There are now over 700 families directly involved with the centre, and interest is still growing.

The Casa del Museo is run on very informal lines. As Mario Vázquez points out, whereas it would be quite impossible for the public to participate in the running of large museums, within a small community such as Santo Domingo this can be made to work very well. Here the local people share in every aspect of the organisation, choosing their own projects and planning the exhibitions, and Mario Vázquez would like eventually to hand the museum over to them entirely, leaving it in their charge. At present there are permanent staff, however, whose job it is to help and advise—without imposing their own ideas or beliefs. Rules are kept to a minimum, and Mario Vázquez explains why:

> In most museums it is forbidden to touch, to smoke, to run or to cry. Almost everything is forbidden except looking at the objects. Of course this is necessary in the formal type of museum,

but it does create a series of barriers. It is as if the visitor were wearing a corset! We want to break down these barriers, and in the Casa del Museo you are allowed to smoke, to cry, to play ball and to dance. You can do whatever you want. As a result there are no inhibitions concerning the objects. You can touch, you can smell, you can draw on the walls. Everything is permitted.

Mario Vázquez and his team aim to show the link between past and present, and to keep people's sense of tradition alive. Themes for recent exhibitions have included health, hygiene and housing. The historic background is given, and the value of traditional methods emphasised. The inhabitants of Santo Domingo are also encouraged to learn about the different customs that prevail in the country areas where many of them grew up. This ensures that small children who are born in the city will not lose touch with the ways of their parents and their ancestors.

Exhibition in the *Casa del Museo* with an altar for the Night of the Dead and a tiny replica on the right of the Aztec 'skull rack'

Continuity with the past is reinforced by temporary exhibitions of artefacts from the Museum of Anthropology. For Mario Vázquez this is one of the most significant aspects of the project:

> You might think we are taking a risk, bringing archaeological pieces to the Casa del Museo without taking any security measures. But we try to trust the community, because I believe that our cultural heritage is not an old stone to be kept locked away in the dark. For me it is something living. And if we are going to succeed in retaining our national identity, we must use our treasures like tools, making them work for us and for the future.

It is ironical that while archaeologists and anthropologists step up their study programmes, the very cultures which interest them are coming under increasing pressure to change. The current president, José Lopez Portillo, has been reported by a US magazine as saying that many Mexicans prefer to remain poor because, being Indian, they wished to remain outside the social and economic mainstream. But Mexico is committed to progress in the interests of the national economy. As new roads are built, as communications improve and as more land is needed for cultivation, Indian communities are bound to be affected. Even the development of the oil wells, which promises to bring such prosperity, may eventually displace the Indians who live on the land.

1 The First Temples

Many archaeologists believe that man first came to the Americas during the last Ice Age, probably about 25,000 BC. A drop in the world's temperature had caused the polar caps to grow in size, locking up increasing quantities of water. As the level of the seas dropped, dry land was exposed between Asia and North America, and across this land-bridge the first early hunters travelled, migrating from north-east Asia. At the end of the Ice Age the glaciers melted, and, as sea levels rose again, the Americas were once more cut off from Asia. From then until the arrival of the Europeans, their cultures and civilisations developed without any proven outside influence. The descendants of these pre-Hispanic peoples, despite local variation, are of the same racial type, and analysis of their blood groups supports the idea that they derive from a small ancestral group likely to have entered the Americas at only one period.

The first Americans were nomadic, hunting animals and gathering wild plants for food. They moved southwards with remarkable speed, fanning out across North, Central and South America. All the skeletons that have been found from the Early Hunting Period indicate that they belonged to the Mongoloid branch of mankind. These early people made use of simple stone tools, but by 10,000 BC more efficient weapons for hunting had been developed, and skilfully-flaked stone points dating from this period have been found throughout the Americas. One of the oldest man-made objects from Mexico is thought to be a flint point, found on the surface of the ground in northern Mexico and once used to tip a hunting spear. Further south, near Santa Isabel Iztápan, slaughtered mammoths, together with the spearheads that killed them, were excavated from the old lake flats. The mammoths had been butchered on the spot with scrapers, obsidian knives and other flint tools that were still lying nearby.

The New World must have seemed like paradise to these hunting people. Large herds of mammoths, mastodons, horses and giant bison roamed through both subcontinents. But around 7000 BC the climate changed, and a period of higher temperatures began. One by one the large game animals perished, and the people had to adapt themselves to a new way of life. With only smaller animals to kill, they began to concentrate more and more on the collection of plant foods. By 6000 BC the people of Central Mexico had taken a step which was to revolutionise the whole course of man's development in the Americas: they had domesticated maize. The ancient strain of maize was tiny in comparison with modern examples, but it was sufficient to provide a regular supply of food which the people themselves could control. Relieved of the need to wander across the plains in search of wild plants and animals, they

Harvesting the maize crop in the mountains of Puebla

began to build up small village communities with mud huts and maize fields. This is a way of life which in many regions has remained unchanged even today.

Maize was and still is the very basis of settled life in Mexico, and with settled life came the beginnings of artistic expression. From about 2000 BC pottery was being made, but it was not until about 1000 BC that the first of the major distinctive cultures emerged. In the hot and tropical lowland swamps of the Gulf Coast, where it rains for the greater part of the year, ceremonial centres began to appear. Massive stone heads, some as much as 9 ft high, were carved out of basalt rock. Stone 'altars' were decorated with figures that were part human and part jaguar. Artificial platforms, mounds and

Olmec altar from the ceremonial centre of La Venta

pyramid-like structures were laid out with formal precision. While Solomon was building the Temple of Jerusalem, the Olmec people were laying the foundations of Mexican civilisation.

The Olmec are one of the great enigmas of Mexican archaeology. Their name, which was given to them by later cultures, means simply 'the people from the land of rubber' — of which the Gulf Coast was a major source. No one knows who they were or where they came from, but they produced the first well-developed art style, and became the great 'mother culture' of Middle America. They appear to have been the originators of hieroglyphic writing in ancient Mexico. They also knew and used a calendar. A number of Olmec objects are incised with hieroglyphs and one, which has become known as Stela C, from Tres Zapotes, is thought to be the monument bearing the oldest date so far deciphered in the New World. The date, in terms of our calendar, corresponds to 31 BC.

The Olmec also built the first major religious centres which were located at San Lorenzo, Tres Zapotes and La Venta. La Venta, perhaps the most important, was built on an island in the middle of the mangrove swamps. An enormous earth pyramid, some 110 ft high dominates the site. It has a unique, fluted form, with a rectangular base measuring approximately 240 ft by 420 ft. Other mounds were clustered in front of it, and interspersed among these were large numbers of monuments sculpted from basalt rock. Four of the large stone heads were found here. Stone does not occur naturally on the island, and since the nearest source of basalt is over eighty miles away, the task of transporting it must have been immense. Some of the blocks are estimated to weigh 40–50 tons, yet somehow the Olmec managed either to float them on rafts, or to

Massive Olmec head over 9 feet high from San Lorenzo

roll them on logs through the dense forests to their sacred island centre.

The layout of La Venta is said to represent the gigantic abstraction of a jaguar, an animal sacred to the Olmec. His features haunt their sculpture which shows strange creatures, part jaguar and part human, with puffy faces like small, fat babies. The upper lips are thick and flared as though snarling, while the mouths are drawn down like those of crying babies. One mutilated carving found at another Olmec site shows a scene which some have interpreted as a jaguar copulating with a woman. It has been suggested that the Olmec may have believed the result of this union to be a race of were-jaguars, which they depicted as baby-faced creatures. As well as carving large stone statues, they also produced exquisite jade figurines, some only eight inches high. Even these small pieces have a distinct and powerful style, and nearly all share the characteristic 'baby-face' and jaguar features. One of the most remarkable finds was a group of sixteen figures placed, as though taking part in a ceremony, in front of six celts (slender bars of jadeite).

Olmec jade figurine with characteristic 'baby face' and jaguar features (height 4¾ inches *cf. colour plate 22*)

Surprisingly, jaguar cults still persist today. Spanish chroniclers, describing what they saw at the time of the Conquest, wrote of the veneration which the Indians had for the jaguar. Many believed it to represent the sun of the night, with its spots calling to mind the stars in the sky. There were numerous dances featuring this animal and imitating its movements. Fray Bernardino de Sahagún, Lopez de Gómara and other Spanish chroniclers described the elaborate masks and costumes which were worn by performers, and which acted as a sort of bridge between the natural world and that of the spirits, bringing to the wearer the animal's attributes.

Despite efforts made by priests after the Conquest to stamp out these dances, the jaguar remains the most impersonated animal in Mexico, and in many Indian communities in different parts of the country the jaguar, popularly but misleadingly known as a tiger, is featured in dances. Most of these continue to celebrate its strength and power, combining this with an agricultural theme and following a strong narrative line. Since the introduction of Christianity, these dances have been integrated by the Indians into the Catholic calendar. They are performed on the principal feast days in honour of the saints and for the amusement of villagers. Outsiders are not normally welcome.

Warrior of the Order of the Jaguar Knights from an Aztec codex

In the rugged state of Guerrero, where so many ancient dances have survived, an unusual version of the Jaguar dance is performed annually by the villagers of Totoltepec. Half a day's walk from the main highway along a bumpy and winding mud track, the village clings to the side of a hill and centres on the large stone church which was built at the height of the Catholic missionary zeal. They celebrate 'Ecce Homo', the Crucified Christ, and before festivities can begin in His honour, dancers take part in a procession to the church to pay their respects to the holy image, followed by villagers bearing candles and armfuls of flowers. When the sacred formalities have been completed, the performers line up outside the church in the hot sunshine, and the villagers gather round to watch the slow unfolding of the pageant, which will last all day. This dramatised dance, interspersed with snatches of dialogue, recounts the exploits and subsequent death of a marauding jaguar who has been invading the fields of the local farmers. They have cleared and prepared their land for cultivation, but the tiger (or jaguar) is undoing all their efforts, and the angry farmers agree to band together and hunt it down.

Accompanied by the music of the flute and drum, played simultaneously in the pre-Conquest tradition by one man, the villager impersonating the jaguar leaps and prances defiantly in front of the farmers, turning somersaults and rushing at his attackers. His costume consists of a shirt and trousers, painted bright yellow and decorated with black circles to simulate the jaguar's markings. His head-dress is also made of painted cloth, stretched over a wooden frame, and embellished with gleaming eyes of mirror, real teeth and a red, protruding leather tongue. In lieu of claws, he carries a long rope which he cracks threateningly as he cavorts around the churchyard, sending flying anyone unwise enough to come too close. His pursuers wear modern jackets and trousers, which soon become covered with a layer of dust. Wide-brimmed palm hats, streaming with colourful ribbons, keep off the heat of the sun. The faces of the hunters are concealed by leather masks with long beards of horsehair and pointed wooden noses. To help them they have a dog, played by another young man of the village. Like the jaguar he wears a cloth head-dress, and he goes by the name of *La Perra Maravilla* or 'The Miracle Dog'.

As the day wears on, the farmers continue to hunt their prey, leaping up and down in parallel rows. Meanwhile the jaguar

The jaguar or 'tiger' dance performed in the village of Totoltepec in Guerrero (*see colour plates 24–8*)

taunts and mocks them, growling from behind his mask and turning innumerable somersaults and cartwheels. The role is so energetic and demanding that on one occasion the dancer who was impersonating the tiger broke his nose while doing a particularly strenuous series of cartwheels, and had to be replaced by a second performer.

The hunt continues to go badly until another dancer, a small boy dressed as a deer, makes his appearance in the church patio. The jaguar kills the deer, and prepares to devour his prey. He is now off his guard and the farmers close in on him, but the jaguar regains his freedom by making a spectacular escape which marks the highlight of the dance. Stretching from the church up into a distant tree is a long rope, and the tiger scrambles along it, spinning around it as he goes, and eventually disappearing into the foliage. The dog, hot on his trail, also launches himself along the rope, and he is followed by the farmers. The hunt ends with the capture and death of the jaguar, and the farmers carry the corpse triumphantly back to the main dancing area. A swarm of vultures, played by village children, close in on the jaguar as if to devour the carcase, and the farmers mime the skinning of it and congratulate themselves on a successful end to the hunt—their fields are now safe from the attacks of the marauding jaguar.

In ancient times the cult of the jaguar, which attributed strange and magical powers to this fierce animal, eventually spread to all parts of Mexico. But, as we have seen, the origins of the cult extend at least as far back as Olmec times on the Gulf Coast. By about 900 BC Olmec influence had reached the Oaxaca Valley of southern Mexico, and even further south into the Maya area. In the central Highlands, groups were slowly coming together in small rural communities, but no elaborate religious centres had as yet been built. Some idea of the way these highland people lived was gained when a remarkable settlement was discovered in 1936 by bricklayers looking for clay near what is now Mexico City. The site has become known as Tlatilco, 'the place where things are hidden'. It dates from 1400 BC to 600 BC, and no less than 340 burials were uncovered by archaeologists.

Thousands of objects have been excavated, many of them figurines of men and women. Some wear loincloths or short

Burial site from Tlatilco as reconstructed in the Mexican Museum of Anthropology

skirts, others appear to be dancing or playing musical instruments. There are hunchbacks, dwarfs and acrobats, as well as little figures who seem to represent shamans or magicians. Some even have two heads. Pottery masks were made in the form of human or animal faces, and vases were modelled in the shape of fish, birds and animals. But perhaps the most startling image was a clay mask divided into two halves. One half shows a human face, and the other a skull. It is one of the oldest representations of death ever found in Mexico, and reveals for the first time the dual conception of life and death, the uniting of the two opposing principles, upon which later religions in Mexico were based.

Among the many objects of local type, a small proportion of items show distinctly Olmec characteristics. Some pots were decorated with jaguar claws, while others showed faces with enlarged, jaguar-like mouths. The Olmec influence had reached Tlatilco by 800 BC, and their strange art style with its snarling 'baby-face' iconography is unmistakably apparent in many of

Pottery mask, half face half skull, from Tlatilco

Pottery figurines from Tlatilco (height 4 to 5 inches)

Circular temple at Cuicuilco *c.* 200 BC

Huehueteotl, the Old God or God of Fire, from Cuicuilco

the figurines. Gradually the small village communities were being replaced by hierarchical societies with priest-rulers who could call on the people to build and maintain sizeable religious centres.

By 200 BC a powerful priestly caste had emerged in the Highlands, and at Cuicuilco one of the first great ceremonial centres was built. The principal feature was a tiered, conical platform made from layers of earth and rubble. It was faced with volcanic rock, and differed from most later pyramids in having a round rather than a square or rectangular plan. With the building of this religious centre came the worship of specific gods. Not surprisingly one of the first was Huehueteotl, the god of fire and of the centre of the earth, for looming on the horizon was Xitli, the volcano which was later to erupt and to pour out molten lava across the whole valley. Huehueteotl was conceived as an old hunchback carrying a brazier on his back, and a small pottery effigy of this god was discovered beneath the rubble at Cuicuilco. Almost identical images have been found throughout Mexico belonging to later cultures.

And so the gods of Mexico began to appear in all their bewildering variety and slowly crystallised into a complete pantheon of gods—among them Huehueteotl, the god of fire; Tlaloc, the rain god; Chalchiuhtlicue, goddess of the waters; the Feathered Serpent, known to later peoples as Quetzalcoatl and revered for his affinities with learning and art. But in all this pantheon there were as yet no gods of war: these were not to appear until the coming of new, fiercer peoples.

Technology was now moving forward. Crude plumb-lines were introduced, and hammers and planes for levelling floors and walls. While the Roman empire was falling into ruin, the first civilisations of Middle America were moving towards their peak. Yet in some ways, their technology was to remain rather backward. Although some children's toys were made with wheels attached to them, no form of wheel was ever put to practical use in ancient Mexico, and metal technology was virtually unknown until after AD 900. All their impressive achievements were to be largely the work of human muscle.

During the last century BC, thirty miles from Cuicuilco, a new religious centre was rising from the plain. It was to become the first great urban centre of Mexico. A thousand years later the Aztec were to call it Teotihuacán, 'the place where men become gods', for they believed it had been built by the gods when the sun and moon were created and the world began. Their legends were written down at the time of the Conquest by the Spanish chroniclers, one of whom, Fray Bernardino de Sahagún, has left us this account:

Wheeled animal figurine from Remojadas, Veracruz

It is told that when all was yet in darkness, when yet no sun had shone and no dawn had broken, the gods gathered themselves together and took council among themselves there at Teotihuacán. They spoke and said among themselves 'Come hither, O gods! Who will carry the burden? Who will take it upon himself to be the sun to bring the dawn?' And upon this, one of them who was there spoke, saying, 'O gods, I shall be the one'. And again the gods spoke: 'And who else?' Thereupon they looked around at one another. Then the gods called to this one. They said to him, 'Thou shalt be the one, Nanauatzin.' He then eagerly accepted the decision, he took it gladly, and he said 'It is well, O gods, you have been good to me'.

On both sides the gods arranged themselves in line. They stood facing and looking toward the youth. And thereupon the gods spoke: 'Take courage, fall, cast thyself into the fire.'

The First Temples 39

General view of Teotihuacán in the Valley of Mexico, which flourished around AD 300

And Nanauatzin, daring all at once, determined, resolved, hardened his heart, and shut firmly his eyes. He had no fear, he did not falter in his fright, he did not turn back. All at once he quickly threw himself into the fire. Thereupon he burned, and his body crackled and sizzled. And when Tecuciztecatl saw that he was already burning, he then afterward cast himself upon the fire. Thereupon he also burned.

When both had cast themselves into the flames, when they had already burned, then the gods sat waiting. When they had been sitting and waiting for a long time, there began the reddening of the dawn. In all directions all around the dawn and light extended.

And when the sun came to rise, when he burst forth, he appeared to be red. He kept swaying from side to side. It was impossible to look into his face, for he blinded one with his light, so intensely did he shine. He issued rays of light from himself. His rays reached in all directions, his brilliant rays penetrated everywhere.

Thus the sun comes forth once and spends the whole day in his work, and the moon undertakes the night's task, he works all night and does his labour at night. . . Thus the ancients thought it to be.

The bones of mammoths, which had perished in the area thousands of years ago, were found by later peoples who came to believe that they belonged to a race of giants. They concluded that they had been the builders of the city, as the same chronicler recorded:

They say it is called Teotihuacán. And when the rulers died, they buried them there. Then they built a pyramid over them . . . and they built the pyramids of the sun and the moon very large, just like mountains. It is not to be believed when it is said that they are made by human hand, for giants still lived there then.

Even as late as the nineteenth century visitors to the site were still baffled by its origins. In the early 1840s W. H. Prescott, the American historian, wrote:

What thoughts must crowd on the mind of the traveller, as he wanders amidst these memorials to the past; as he treads over the ashes of the generations who reared these colossal fabrics, which take us from the present into the very depths of time! But who were the builders? A nation has passed away—powerful, populous and well advanced in refinement as attested by their monuments—but it has perished without a name!

Archaeologists are beginning to solve the mystery of Teotihuacán. It was not just a religious centre but a true city with houses, palaces, temples and great plazas. Building started around 100 BC, and by AD 350 it was a flourishing metropolis. A new priestly caste governed society and promoted learning, actively supporting crafts and encouraging the worship of the gods, particularly of a Rain God and a Feathered Serpent.

Teotihuacán is dominated by two immense pyramids that have become known as the Pyramid of the Sun and the Pyramid of the Moon. They were built to serve as a base or foundation for the temples which crowned their summits. A long avenue, the so-called 'Avenue of the Dead', runs south from the Pyramid of the Moon, stretching over two miles. On either side of the avenue are the remains of platforms, smaller pyramids, courts and palaces. The rest of the city was divided into districts, some for craftsmen and others residential. The poorer part of the population lived in clusters of small wooden huts on the periphery. By AD 300 the whole site covered an

Pyramid of the Sun at Teotihuacán, over 200 feet high (*see also colour plate 16*)

area of more than seventy-four acres, and the estimated population was about 45,000.

The main structures were built of rubble, faced with stone. Hewn from the rock with wooden wedges and hammers, the stones were then cut and dressed with chisels and polishers. The masons employed stone plumbs, polishers or planes for the floors and walls, as well as cords, rollers and earthen ramps. The buildings were sometimes decorated with stone mosaic work and usually finished with a layer of lime plaster or stucco, to which paint and stone mosaics might be added. In the plaza known as the *Ciudadela*, excavations revealed that one of the buildings concealed the remains of an earlier one beneath it. A six-tiered step pyramid was uncovered with panels, displaying monumental images of serpents, their bodies adorned with feathers, and their heads protruding from a feathered ruff. Alternating with these figures are grotesque sculptures with huge fangs and two circles on the forehead. They are generally thought to represent Tlaloc, the Rain God, while others believe that they belong to a corn deity. The whole temple has been named after Quetzalcoatl, the Plumed Serpent, and it is thought that his may have been an important cult at Teotihuacán.

Many of the other temples and houses are decorated with frescoes. The basic colours of red, green, blue, yellow and black were extracted from minerals, and ground in mortars or on palettes to provide the various pigments. Most of the frescoes follow strict rules of style and form. Stiffly drawn figures are shown taking part in religious rituals concerned with agricul-

Temple of Quetzalcoatl, the Plumed Serpent, at Teotihuacán

Wall painting from Teotihuacán showing a jaguar with a feathered headdress

Funerary mask covered with a mosaic of turquoise and red shells

ture, fertility and rain. The image of the jaguar appears, wearing vast feathered headdresses and blowing sea-shell trumpets. The rather static nature of these frescoes is in sharp contrast, however, with a mural which is to be found in an outlying area called Tepantitla. The scene, thought to represent the Paradise of the Rain Gods, shows lively little human figures singing and playing in an enchanted garden. They are surrounded by butterflies and flowering trees and above them Tlaloc, the Rain God, looks down, trailing large drops of water from his fingers.

The pottery and sculpture found at Teotihuacán is extremely elegant and refined. Austere stone masks were made with widely-set oval eyes and gently curving, slightly open mouths. A rare example is completely covered with tiny pieces of turquoise mosaic, with inlaid eyes of mother of pearl and burnished obsidian. Pottery was perhaps the most important craft, and alongside their more ordinary clay vessels these early people produced an extremely fine ware known as Thin Orange. All the objects from this site have great grace and serenity, and the faces were shown as calm and reflective.

Although most pottery was made by hand, they developed in

Mural showing the paradise of Tlaloc, the Rain God, from the painted palace of Tepantitla, Teotihuacán

the later period a system of mass production, using moulds to produce hundreds of votive figurines, perhaps for sale to pilgrims. They built up peaceful trading links with peoples as far away as the Gulf Coast of Mexico and the Pacific Coast. In return for their pottery, they acquired conch and other shells which they used as ornaments, or turned into musical instruments. They also produced various items of clothing made from cotton or the fibre of the maguey cactus, using looms and spindles as well as needles and bodkins. Paintings show that the men wore a loin-cloth and the women a tunic and underskirt.

Sadly, no books of any sort have survived from Teotihuacán, if indeed they ever existed; although it is thought that some form of writing may have been in use both ritually and administratively. A few isolated glyphs have been found on pottery and in the frescoes, but there is nothing which tells us why this sophisticated and gentle culture came to an end. It had become the dominant culture of the Central Highlands, exerting considerable influence over neighbouring peoples. Yet there is no evidence of a warrior class, and no signs of any military fortifications have been found. By about AD 650 the

Pottery funerary mask with characteristic oval eyes

Teotihuacán culture had begun to decline. No more buildings were erected, and the arts became coarse and decadent. One theory suggests that the priests had somehow lost control and that the economy collapsed. Whatever the reason, bands of less advanced people began to invade the area, and the buildings fell into ruin.

But on the Gulf Coast, a religious centre that had grown up at the same time as Teotihuacán and with which trading relationships had been established, continued to flourish. El Tajín was built slightly north of the Olmec area and was the ceremonial centre of the Totonac people. Because of heavy rains and tropical storms, archaeologists can only excavate for a few weeks each year and progress is slow and costly. The ruins are scattered over several thousand acres and much of the site is still buried beneath dense tropical vegetation. The main groups of monuments and mounds cover an area of about forty thousand square yards which is divided into two parts, the first lying in a small valley and the second, known as Tajín Chico, 'lesser Tajín', being built upon an elevation artificially levelled to form a terrace.

El Tajín was the centre of a remarkable and unique architectural style. Nearly all the buildings are decorated with variations and combinations of fret patterns, projecting corners and niches. The niches were never intended to hold anything, but were a device to produce a play of light and shade. The most striking building is in fact called the Pyramid of the Niches and here the niche becomes an architectural motif in its own right. The pyramid rises in seven tiers to a height of sixty feet and the vertical walls of each layer are faced with slabs of sedimentary rock and decorated with square niches. Complex mathematical theories have been put forward to explain them and some are beginning to gain currency. The temple has 365 niches, and since the solar calendar of 365 days was known in ancient Mexico it is thought that the two were in some way related. A single stairway climbs to a small sanctuary at the top, flanked by balustrades embellished with a step-and-fret motif.

The whole site is surrounded by low hills and set in a region where tropical storms are frequent and violent. This probably explains why the Totonac called their sacred centre El Tajín. For in the Totonac language Tajín means 'the place of lightning and thunder.' Although the site has long been abandoned the Totonac people still live in the area, scattered in small

Pyramid of the Niches at El Tajín on the Gulf Coast (*see colour plate 14*)

communities throughout this hot and humid territory. They are the largest Indian group to inhabit the Gulf of Mexico and according to the latest figures they number 150,000, of whom 50,000 speak only Totonac.

The Totonac villages are isolated and many still have no electricity or running water. Their houses, like most Indian houses, are made of wood or mud brick with palm or tiled roofs. Traditionally they are windowless and inside there are just one or two simple rooms, with areas for cooking and sleeping. They have earthen floors and in the cooking area pots are balanced over an open fire. Furniture is minimal, with clothing and most belongings suspended from rough hooks or bars. Cradles for the smaller children are also suspended from the roof. In the corner

Above Totonac traditional costume from Ecatlán, Puebla

Right Totonac farmer in Ecatlán drying coffee beans

of every kitchen is the grinding stone whose style and function has remained unchanged since those early times when maize was first cultivated.

Traditional wear for Totonac men consists of white shirts and baggy trousers made of white cotton, while the women wear wrap-around skirts held in place by a waist-sash with a sleeveless top of pre-Hispanic origin called a '*quechquemitl*' which is worn over a European-type blouse. Most Totonac are poor and live by subsistence farming, growing maize, beans, squash and vanilla on their small plots of land. Some Totonac hire themselves out to Mexican landowners as day labour, earning about £1 a day, or less if it rains and work is broken off. Some also engage in small commercial enterprises of their own, picking fruit on other people's land and then selling it at the local market.

Although they are now all Roman Catholic, many traits of the old Totonac religion persist in mountain areas. Rituals are held in caves to honour the old gods who embody the natural forces: the Thunder Beings, the Owner of the Forest, the Owner of the Water and the Owner of the Harvest. The earth is still thought of as a living force. In some places it is believed that the world is flat and the heavens domed, and that when the sun sets it passes under the earth. They consider the universe to be divided into horizontal layers: at the top is the Sun and below is the Moon. When the Sun and Moon quarrel there is an eclipse.

Four bearers hold up the earth at each corner, and an earthquake results if one of them shifts his weight.

In common with many other ancient Mexican cultures, many Totonac believe that the present era is that of the fifth 'Sun', or world, four others having preceded it and been destroyed. The next 'cleansing of time' will be in the year 2000. Others believe that the world will only end 'when birds have red heads; when dogs lose their tails; when ants give off their poison; when squash are made of water. And these things will only come about when the sun and the moon appear together, shining with equal brightness.' According to their myths, before the coming of the Sun the world belonged to the 'ancient ones'. The Sun-elect was conceived when a woman accidentally swallowed a bright trinket which she found in the water. She died giving birth and the infant Sun emerged from her navel. He grew to manhood extremely quickly and then built a great fire into which (like Nanauatzin of old), he threw himself. As he soared upwards, he slowly turned into the Sun. With the appearance of the Sun, the 'ancient ones' were turned into 'stones, trees and all the animals; the mortars, grinding stones and the cooking pots'. One day, they say, when this era ends there will be no more light and these creatures and objects will resume their former identity and eat mankind.

A few Totonac still visit El Tajín. They come as their ancestors before them, to perform an ancient ritual. Five men dressed in ceremonial costume climb to the top of an enormous pole to take part in the 'Voladores' dance. Performed in villages throughout the area to honour the Roman Catholic saints, the dance is still an act of worship, seen as a way of ensuring a successful harvest, a good rainfall and the harmonious succession of the four seasons.

The ritual begins long before the day of the fiesta. The elders go into the forest in search of a tree, and once one is selected they encircle it, dancing round it many times. They then group themselves into the shape of a cross and address the four cardinal points, which have been marked out with lighted torches. Men with axes then enter the central arena and fell the tree. It is stripped of its foliage and bark, and dignitaries from the community arrive, entrusted with the special task of dragging the tree to the spot where it is to be erected. Into the hole which will receive it, a chicken, eggs, alchohol, and sherry with aniseed are dropped as an offering to the god of the earth.

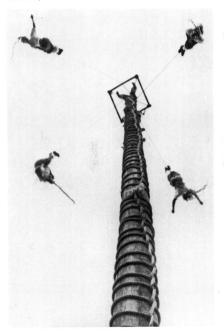

The *Voladores* Dance: four Totonac men fly towards the ground, while a fifth perches precariously on a tiny platform on top of the pole (*see also colour plates 29 and 30*)

The *Voladores* dance as shown in an ancient Mexican codex

Around the selected tree, which may be up to eighty feet high, thick vines are tied to form a scaling ladder. A small revolving platform about two feet across is fixed to the top, and below it four ropes, one for each of the 'flyers', hang down. The ropes are wound round the pole and the platform in such a way that they will unwind as the platform revolves. The dance itself is spectacular. The five performers climb to the top of the pole and huddle together on the tiny platform. One, playing a pipe and drum, performs a hair-raising dance in the middle of the platform while the others each take one of the ropes and tie it around their waist. At a given moment in the music the four men hurl themselves off into the air. As the platform rotates, their ropes gradually unwind and they seem to 'fly' towards the ground.

The man at the top, they say, represents the sun, and the four swinging round him the seasons of the year. Each is supposed to circle the pole thirteen times before reaching the ground, and the total of fifty-two turns symbolises the passage of a century in the ancient Totonac calendar. Before the Spanish Conquest the *Voladores* dance had spread to most communities and was performed throughout Mexico. Although the Spaniards tried hard to stop the ceremony, it continued. Today it has lost most of its old meaning but it does retain a religious significance, combining elements of past belief with Catholicism.

One sacred ritual which the Spanish priests did succeed in stamping out was the Ball Game. El Tajín has no less than seven ball courts. They are little more than open-ended corridors up to 200 ft long, flanked by either vertical or sloping walls. Ball courts have been found all over Mexico and they vary considerably in shape and size. Most have end walls, giving the court a shape like two Ts placed end to end; some have stone rings or markers fixed in the walls halfway down on either side of the court; others have markers set in the floor of the court. The game is thought to have been invented by the Olmec. It was closely associated with worship and ritual, and all the courts have a temple built beside them.

Opinions differ as to how the game was actually played, even though the early Spanish chroniclers have left us one or two eyewitness accounts:

> There came a great multitude of lords and gentlemen and they played it with great joy and delight. There were players who

were so skilled that in a whole hour they never let the ball stop, hitting it with the haunches, never with the hand, foot or arm, counting it a fault to touch it with the hands or other parts of the body, with the exception of the haunches and the knees, and so skilled and excellent were some players that not only did kings esteem them but they also gave them entry to their house and court, honouring them with special tokens.

The ball was of the size of those for wind, but it was heavier because it was made from a certain rubber which comes from trees which grew in the hot lands. When this kind of tree is punctured, thick white drops come out and these immediately coagulate; when treated they become black. These balls bounce much more than those of wind. You have only to let it fall from your hand to the ground for it to bounce up much higher, and it gives one bounce then another and another and maybe more and these bounces grow less of their own accord.

Ball game illustrated in 16th-century codex known as the Codex Magliabecchiano

The game was apparently fast, rough and tiring, and on occasions players died from exhaustion or physical injury. It was not uncommon for games to last several days and people followed the course of play with hot enthusiasm, betting heavily on the outcome. Spectators sat in rows along the walls that surrounded the Ball Court. The players were divided into two teams and a section of each team occupied the lateral side of the court, attempting to stop the ball from going out of bounds. The best players from both teams faced each other at mid-court, somehow keeping the ball in motion by hitting it

'Yoke'

Palma

Hacha

with their hips. Despite what we learn from the chroniclers, some accounts suggest that the use of knees and elbows was also allowed. The game obviously had many variations. When it was played in a court with a stone ring or hoop it is thought that a definite victory was gained only by hitting the ball through the stone ring—an extraordinarily difficult feat considering the height of the ring and the limited means by which it was permitted to propel the ball. But since many of the courts, including all those at El Tajín, did not have stone rings, there were obviously other ways of scoring the game.

Players wore heavy belts, sometimes made of deerskin, from which hung other pieces of deerskin to protect the hips. Leather pads covered the thighs, the knees and the hands and the entire uniform was finely worked with decorative, ritually symbolic motifs. The people of El Tajín used the objects from the Ball Game as the inspiration for some of their finest stone carvings. Stone replicas of the heavy protective belts worn by the players took the form of U-shaped 'Yokes' and were intricately carved with convoluted scrolls and human faces. There are also stone replicas of other paraphernalia associated with the ball game. These include the *palma*, which seems to represent a type of protector; and the *hachas*, thin stone heads, are thought by some to be markers placed in the courts to score the game. The *hachas* are also referred to as 'axes', and are now believed to have some connection with the final rituals of the game. For what the Spaniards had not realised was that most of the games ended in death by decapitation.

At El Tajín there is a frieze in one of the Ball Courts, which graphically illustrates those last harrowing moments. The court has magnificent reliefs along both sides, many showing ceremonies in the court itself with all the players wearing the appropriate paraphernalia. But in one corner the spiny, fleshless skeleton of Mictlantecuhtli, the God of Death, looks on as the central figure is held down on the sacrifical altar to be beheaded by his opponent with an axe. Some believe that it was the captain of the winning, not the losing, side who was sacrificed— honoured by being sent as a messenger to the gods.

In southern Mexico, at the Mayan site of Chichén Itzá, there is a similar frieze in the Ball Court. One of the players has been executed, and from his neck pours blood in the form of seven serpents which in turn become flowers, the symbols of fertility. Beneath the central flowering plant, a skull representing the

God of Death waits to gather up his offering. For the ancient Mexican, sacrifice ensured continuity of life, and worship of death involved worship of life. Just as the day struggled with the night, so life struggled with death. According to one Spanish chronicler, the tenth month of the indigenous calendar was the time for the feast of the dead, when solemn ceremonies took place in which many men were slaughtered. Offerings were laid around the sacrifical altar while the young men, dressed in elaborate costumes of feathers and jewels, danced in attendance.

Today, death is as vivid to the Mexicans as it was to their ancestors. All Souls' Day, the day on which the Catholic Church pays homage to the departed, has been claimed by the Mexicans and renamed the 'Day of the Dead'. It is a national holiday on which all over Mexico people visit the cemeteries to tidy graves, repaint them and entertain the spirits of the departed with candles and music. The graves are decorated with yellow marigolds, the 'flowers of the dead', for in ancient Mexico yellow was the colour of death, symbolising the south where the dead were said to go. The pre-Hispanic incense called *copal* is burnt while offerings of food and drink are placed on the gravestones.

Mictlantecuhtli, God of Death: terracotta figure from the Gulf Coast

At this festival children are given toys in the form of skulls and skeletons, some of them even articulated so that they dance when you pull a string. Sugar skulls are presented to friends and relatives, with their names written on the forehead. Clay models of burials and weddings are produced in which all the participants are skeletons—carts are drawn by skeleton horses and filled with skeleton passengers, musical instruments are played by skeleton musicians, skeleton brides are followed by festive skeletons in modern dress.

Skeletons at a dance—an example of the humorous way in which death is often viewed in Mexico

Among the Indians in rural areas there is a strong belief that at this season the dead have heavenly permission to visit their relatives still on earth, and elaborate preparations are made to give them a fitting reception. The Totonac Indians set up magnificent altars decked with yellow flowers and covered with mounds of specially cooked food. Large loaves of bread are baked for the departed and are surrounded by all their favourite dishes and drinks. The Totonac believe that the invisible but hovering dead will return and partake of the aroma of the food. When it is thought that the dead have had their fill, the living settle down to eat the rest.

The cult of the dead did not reach its height in Ancient

Mexico until after AD 900, with the emergence of the great war gods, Tezcatlipoca and Huitzilopochtli. About AD 600 the great ceremonial centres of the 'Classic' period, such as Teotihuacán, declined, and throughout Mexico there was a state of unrest and confusion. El Tajín was one of the few centres to survive the great upheaval. Elsewhere, the intellectual hierarchy of the older cultures was replaced by a class of tough, professional warriors. War became the rule of the day, for the gods were now hungry for the taste of human blood.

Totonac celebrating the Night of the Dead around a traditional altar

2 The Empire Builders

During the period of chaos and decadence in the Central Highlands that followed the decline of Teotihuacán, marauding tribes poured into the Valley of Mexico, vying with one another for political supremacy. A new religious site grew up a hundred miles to the south of Teotihuacán, strategically placed on a large hill which was artificially reshaped with stepped terraces, defensive ditches, ramparts and other kinds of fortifications. It was for some time thought to be closely linked with the culture of Teotihuacán, but a study of the architecture, sculpture and pottery made after excavations revealed that it also had strong connections with the Maya culture in the far south, as well as with the peoples of the valley of Oaxaca.

The site has become known as Xochicalco, 'the place of flowers', and it is still something of an archaeological mystery.

General view of Xochicalco, the 'Place of Flowers'

Within its fortifications there are plazas, temples, altars and ball-courts. The principal temple is the Pyramid of the Plumed Serpent, whose lower part is decorated with plumed serpents not unlike those at Teotihuacán. The coils of the serpents' bodies, however, are surrounded by glyphs, and by dignitaries sitting cross-legged and wearing elaborate head-dresses. These seated figures are very like those found on Mayan bas-reliefs. Maya influence is also evident in some of the ball courts which, like the Mayan courts, are in the shape of a capital 'I' with two stone rings embedded halfway along the walls.

Hieroglyphs and symbolic signs feature prominently on the main buildings, and throughout the site there are caves which appear to have been adapted for astronomical observation. The entrance to one of the largest of these caves is through an irregular opening in the limestone. Inside there is a low natural vault with a coloured stucco floor. This appears to be the entrance hall and at one end a narrow passage leads to a spacious chamber. Here, in a corner, is a sort of funnel or chimney with a diameter of about two yards tapering towards the daylight far above. Its function is uncertain, but at the time

Details from the frieze decorating the temple of the Plumed Serpent at Xochicalco: *above* Seated cross-legged figure reminiscent of Mayan bas-reliefs; *below* Plumed Serpent

Impressive ball court at Xochicalco,
measuring 90 yds long

of the equinoxes the sun shines directly into this shaft.
Archaeologists now believe that Xochicalco may have been a
meeting place for astronomers and emissaries who came from
all over ancient Mexico to make calendrical correlations. All
the Middle-American peoples used a rather complicated
calendar which involved the meshing of the days of a 260-day
Almanac Year with those of the 365-day Solar Year. Only
once in 52 years would a particular day in one meet a
particular day in the other and by this means any date could be
placed within a single 52-year cycle. This is nowadays called
the 'Calendar Round'. Calculations by this method were
obviously limited to a 52-year period. The Maya, however,
developed a system called the 'Long Count', enabling them to
calculate longer periods which involved the counting of days
which had elapsed from a chosen date in the past, and was a
more exact way of expressing dates (see also page 128).

At Xochicalco one group of dates seems to record the
adjustment of the calendar at this site to make it accord with

those of other areas. Glyphs using the numbering system employed by the Central Highland people are shown opposite glyphs of the Maya system. In the middle there is a figure who appears to be binding the dates together. The Spanish chronicler Fray Bernardino de Sahagún refers to a people who settled in 'the place of the bird-serpent'. There 'they composed the count of the days, of the nights and of the years' which continued in use until the time of the Spanish Conquest. He goes on to say that some groups left 'the place of the bird-serpent', travelling through level country or high barren plains to discover new lands where they founded a new city. These historic references suggest that the 'place of the bird-serpent' could have been Xochicalco. Archaeologists are now convinced that it was in some way a bridge between the old Classic era of Teotihuacán, and the new warlike era which was about to erupt. In fact Xochicalco seems to have contributed directly to the formation of the next great culture to appear in the Valley of Mexico—the powerful Toltec.

By the tenth century, the Toltec had established themselves as the new dominant people, built a large empire and introduced human sacrifice on a vast scale. Although they are one of the first peoples to be mentioned in the historical records of the Valley of Mexico, the references to them are so confusing, their customs and achievements so wrapped in mystery, that even today scholars are baffled by the contradictory evidence.

According to the Annals of Cuauhtitlan, a fourteenth-century Aztec chronicle, the Toltec first established themselves at Culhuacan. Led by their chief, Mixcoatl, they worshipped Tezcatlipoca, the 'Smoking Mirror', who encouraged the practice of human sacrifice. Mixcoatl met a local maiden who bore him a son, Ce Acatl Topiltzin. She died soon after giving birth and Mixcoatl himself was killed by his brother who wanted to seize power. His son Topiltzin was brought up at Xochicalco by the priests who worshipped Quetzalcoatl, the Plumed Serpent. When Topiltzin reached manhood he vowed to avenge his father's death. He returned to Culhuacan, killed his uncle, took over the leadership of the people and eventually led them to the site on which Tula would be built, and from which the Toltec Empire would grow.

Topiltzin was to become one of the most famous legendary figures in all Mexican history. He abhorred human sacrifice and tried to introduce the peaceful cult of Quetzalcoatl. But later peoples were to transform him into a new version of Quetzalcoatl himself, a deity combining two aspects, man and god. To the confusion of modern scholars, the Toltec ruler was transformed into Quetzalcoatl, the benefactor of mankind, the civilising god who had invented and bestowed upon humanity all useful and beautiful arts.

The chronicle goes on to tell us that at first all the people in Tula were wealthy and happy. Quetzalcoatl reigned over them and everywhere there was abundance and happiness. Maize was plentiful, and cotton grew out of the earth already brightly coloured in reds and blues and even spotted like the jaguar. There were unlimited supplies of gold and precious stones and marvellous singing birds of all colours.

Quetzalcoatl fasted, did penance and prayed. He sacrificed snakes and birds, and called on the gods to continue to bestow their bounty. Repeatedly the evil spirits tried to persuade him to offer human sacrifice and repeatedly he refused, for he loved his people, the Toltec, and did not wish to kill them. This angered the evil spirits who longed for the slaying of men. Disguised as sorcerers and led by Tezcatlipoca, who rejoiced in man's misfortunes, they plotted against Quetzalcoatl.

'We must make him abandon his city so that we may live there', they said. 'Let us give him *pulque* wine to drink. Let us corrupt him so that he no longer enjoys divine favour.' Slowly, Tezcatlipoca and his followers undermined Quetzalcoatl with their evil schemes. They tricked him into getting drunk, into forgetting his penance, his fasting and his prayer. He became a sad, drunken wreck: 'Oh miserable that I am. My body has become a thing of clay, and I only have base desires.' Humiliated and ashamed, he decided to leave the city. He commanded his people to hide all their possessions, 'all our gladness and riches, all our finery and wealth'. He destroyed his house and his works of art, converted the cotton plants into cacti, beckoned the sweet singing birds to follow him and abandoned Tula, turning his kingdom into a desert.

Quetzalcoatl set out with his followers in the direction of the Gulf Coast. There, according to one version, he put to sea on a raft formed of serpents. He journeyed to the east from where one day he promised to return. He was said to be fair-skinned with a dark beard and when, five hundred years later, such a figure landed on the shores of Mexico it was believed that Quetzalcoatl had at last returned.

How much historical fact lies behind the legend of the flight of Quetzalcoatl? Topiltzin was almost certainly a real person, born either in AD 935 or 947. Some years after the founding of Tula, he came into conflict with the devotees of the fierce god of war, Tezcatlipoca. One theory suggests they had become irritated with the pacifism of their leader, a man who encouraged the arts and learning and who was against war. After a violent power struggle, Topiltzin and his followers were forced to flee the city.

In the far south, Mayan accounts speak of the arrival around AD 987, of Mexican conquerors. Their leader was called Kukulcan, which in the Maya language means 'Plumed Serpent'. This account is supported by archaeological evidence in the Mayan sites of the Yucatán, where there is a sudden and dramatic change in the architecture and art styles: many of the new buildings and carvings are similar to those found far away in Tula.

The Toltec capital of Tula lies about fifty miles north of what is now Mexico City. At first glance is seems to be rather small, but only the main group of buildings have so far been restored. Unexcavated mounds stretch over a wide area. The architecture is quite different from that of the Classic period, and reflects the increasing preoccupation with violence and war. Temple walls are decorated with warriors, jaguars and serpents swallowing human hearts. Curious statues known as 'chacmools' were placed in front of the altars, symbolising the 'divine messengers' who carried offerings to the gods. They are carved in the form of reclining figures with raised heads, and on their stomachs they bear a large receptacle in which the sacrifical offerings were placed.

Stone *chacmool* figure from Tula—the ceremonial centre of the warlike Toltec

Tula is dominated by a large pyramid, built in five tiers. On the top is a spacious platform on which a temple once stood, the temple roof being given additional support by the introduction of several free-standing columns. The four massive supports of the front row were carved into colossal figures of warriors, over fifteen feet high. Each carries a spear-thrower in the right hand and a bundle of spears in the left, and their immense bodies are covered with almost every detail of their dress and insignia. They were originally painted and their eyes and mouths decorated with inlay.

The four sides of the pyramid are decorated with bas-reliefs of prowling jaguars and coyotes, symbolising the warrior orders

Massive warriors of stone over 15 feet high on the summit of the pyramid at Tula (*See also colour plate 17*)

upon which the strength of the empire depended. Interspersed with these are terrifying images of eagles eating human hearts and strange composite beasts thought to represent Quetzalcoatl. An adjoining wall, over 130 ft long, is carved with snakes swallowing human skeletons.

From their capital at Tula, the Toltec ruled over much of northern and central Mexico. Led by their bloodthirsty god of war, Tezcatlipoca, they established an empire dominated by brutality and human sacrifice, ideas which were later to be adopted by the greatest empire builders of them all: the Aztec.

One tribe who came under Toltec and later Aztec rule were the Otomí, whose descendants still live near Tula. The Otomí Indians were originally a nomadic tribe who came down from the deserts of the north. Today they number over 300,000, many of whom still speak only the Otomí language. After the Spanish conquest they were encouraged to stay in the area, for the Spaniards wished to ensure a submissive, settled, agricultural population in a region still subject to raids of nomads from the north. Some of the Otomí now live in areas where the land is more fertile and where they can grow crops to sell, but a large number still live in the harsh, semi-desert region near Tula, called the Valley of the Mezquital. There is a shortage of land and a rapidly growing population, and scattered throughout this barren landscape, the Otomí lead an impoverished existence.

Their houses are small, dark and windowless and nearly all work is done outside. But although the land is arid and infertile, the Otomí have adapted themselves in a most remarkable way to their harsh environment. The *maguey* or agave cactus is at the centre of their economy. Since the Otomí first appeared in Mexico over a thousand years ago, they have always depended on the *maguey* cactus for their livelihood. Sixty-five per cent of families who live in the Valley support themselves entirely from its exploitation.

The cactus grows wild and is also widely cultivated in special 'cactus fields' by taking cuttings of the small cacti which grow at the base of the fully grown plants. In one way or another every bit of the cactus is used by the Otomí. Their houses are often built from its leaves and stalks, and the dried thorns provide nails for carpentry and needles for sowing. Tufts of cactus fibre are used for washing the pots and pans and the cactus pulp is used as soap. The hearts are roasted and eaten,

Details from the frieze decorating the base of the pyramid at Tula: *top* Coyote *above* Eagles devouring human hearts

Otomí woman spinning *ixtle* or cactus fibre.

and part of the leaf is bent to form a vessel for drinking. Even the larvae that live on the plant are eaten as a special delicacy.

But perhaps its most important use is in the making of two products which have become a vital part of the Otomí economy: *pulque* wine and *ixtle*. *Ixtle* is a thread spun from the fibres extracted from fleshy cactus leaves when they are broken down. The spun yarn is made into rope and string as well as being woven into coarse cloth. Before the Spanish conquest most Indian clothing was made from cactus fibres, for only the rich were able to wear cotton. *Pulque* is an alcoholic drink which has been made in Mexico for over a thousand years, and it is thought to have been invented by the Otomí Indians. In the sixteenth century the Spanish chronicler, Sahagún, recorded how it was made:

> The *maguey* cactus was scraped out, the bountiful *maguey* from which *aguamiel* [the sap] comes. The first to discover the art of scraping was a woman named Mayahuel. But the first to discover the stalk, the root with which the *pulque* is fermented, was a man named Pantecatl.

The making of *pulque* is in fact a rather more complicated process than this account suggests. It takes from five to seven years for a plant to mature. A flowering woody stem then appears, indicating that the plant is ready for 'milking'. The centre of the plant is scraped, which induces it to secrete a sweet sap to cover the wound. The sap is extracted with a long gourd and poured into barrels or leather bottles. This is sometimes drunk as honey-water but more often it is turned into *pulque* wine. The fermenting process takes place in immense cowhide troughs suspended from rectangular wooden frames. The operation is set in motion by introducing some highly fermented *pulque* into the new sap. If it is only being made for home consumption, small pots can be used instead of the huge troughs. *Pulque* is still so widely drunk that vast quantities are produced and transported to market in hogs' bladders.

Pulque wine is extremely potent, and in ancient Mexico there were strict laws governing its consumption. During feasts only the old and those who were no longer useful to the community were permitted to drink it. There were certain days, particularly those on which the dead were remembered, when all might consume the powerful liquid. This was the drink which had led to Quetzalcoatl's fleeing Tula and leaving it in the hands of the

1 Early morning at the weekly Zapotec market of Tlacolula in the Oaxaca Valley (*p.93*).

2 & 3 *Above*: Lacandón man from the lakeside community of Najá, Chiapas. *Right*: Lacandón family outside their house in Najá, Chiapas (*p. 137*).

4 Traditional dress as worn in the mountains of the Mixteca, Oaxaca (*p. 114*)

5 & 6 *Left*: Huichol couple by their maize field near San Andrés Cohamiata, Jalisco (*p. 197*). *Above*: Face-painting with *peyote* symbols during the *peyote* festival, Jalisco (*p. 218*).

7 & 8 *Left*: Nahua family group from the village of Zoatecpan in the hills of Puebla. *Above*: Nahua baby being carried in the traditional way in Cuetzalan, Puebla (*pp. 80ff.*).

9 & 10 Palenque, built by the Maya *c* AD 700 in the rainforest of Chiapas. *Above*: The Palace. *Right*: The Temple of the Foliated Cross (*p. 145*).

'Not for ever on the earth . . .

11 The Pyramid of the Magician at Uxmal, a flourishing Maya centre on the Yucatán peninsula *c* AD 900 (*p. 153*).

12 & 13 *Below left*: The Temple of the Warriors at Chichén Itzá, reflecting the merging of Toltec and Maya traditions, *c* AD 1000. *Below*: Feathered serpents flanking the entrance to the temple (*p. 157*).

. . . only a short time here'

14 The Pyramid of the Niches at El Tajín, on the Gulf Coast, the ceremonial centre of the Totonac (*p. 46*).

15 General view of Monte Albán, the Zapotec centre built high in the hills of Oaxaca (*pp. 89ff.*).

16 The Pyramid of the Sun at Teotihuacán, the immense ceremonial centre in the Vally of Mexico which reached its height *c* AD 300 (*p. 42*).

17 Tula, about 50 miles from Teotihuacán, built by the Toltec *c* AD 900 (*p.61*).

Preparing to extract sap from the *maguey* cactus to make *pulque*

bloodthirsty devotees of the 'Smoking Mirror'.

The Otomí lived under Toltec rule for over 200 years. About AD 1100, however, Tula came to a dramatic end. Quite why is still something of a mystery but all the evidence indicates that the fall was sudden and total. The ceremonial halls were burnt to the ground and the serpent wall smashed. One theory suggests that the city had been weakened by a disastrous series of droughts and internal conflicts, and was then attacked by wild nomads who had come down from the north.

In the confusion that followed the collapse of the Toltec Empire successive waves of hunters and warriors migrated to the Valley from the north. They mingled with the survivors of the Toltec, and soon villages and towns grew up, adopting the more civilised way of life of the already-settled communities. Local dialects were abandoned in favour of Nahuatl, the language spoken by the Toltec, and the ever-expanding towns and cities began fighting for supremacy.

Into this world of political intrigue came a poor ragged tribe with no political leaders other than their tribal chieftains. They called themselves the Azteca, in memory of Aztlán, 'the place of herons', where their wanderings were said to have begun. The civilised groups already living in the Valley of Mexico considered them barbarians, and refused to let them settle. They were driven on from one place to another, but took comfort from the prophecy of their god Huitzilopochtli:

The God Huitzilopochtli as shown in the Aztec codex known as Telleriano-Remensis

The legendary journey taken by the Aztec as illustrated in the Codex Telleriano-Remensis

Go at once and seek out the *tenochtli* cactus upon which an eagle stands in his joy. It is there that we shall fix ourselves. It is there that we shall rule, that we shall wait, that we shall meet the various nations and that with our arrow and our shield we shall overthrow them. Our city shall be there. There where the eagle circles and spreads his wings and eats, there where swims the fish and there where the serpent is devoured.

According to their legend, they travelled for hundreds of years before finally reaching their destination:

They saw the eagle poised on a cactus, eating the serpent and their god called: 'It is here.' And they wept, crying: 'At last we have been worthy. With astonishment we have seen the sign. Our city shall be here.'

The site consisted of a few swampy islands in Lake Texcoco, 7000 ft above sea level. It was such a dismal spot that none of the more civilised peoples in the Valley had wanted it. There was no arable land, so the Aztec piled up mud from the bottom of the lake onto rafts made of rushes, and planted willow trees to keep these 'floating gardens' in place. Encouraged by their god, Huitzilopochtli—the god of war, they became fierce warriors. By 1367 they had become mercenaries for the most powerful kingdom on the mainland, the Tepanec, ruled by Tezozomoc. As, one by one the peoples in the Valley of Mexico fell to the joint forces of Tezozomoc and his allies, the Aztec were rewarded with a share in the loot, and from the Tepanec they began learning techniques of statecraft and empire building. They also absorbed the cultural heritage of the Valley peoples, particularly that of the Toltec, whose glorification of war appealed to the fierce, fighting Aztec.

In 1426 Tezozomoc was succeeded by his son Maxtlatzin. The new Tepanec ruler felt threatened by the growing power of the Aztec in their island kingdom and began interfering in their affairs. The Aztec resented this, and under their ruler Itzcoatl took up arms against the 'Tyrant Maxtla'. A year later Maxtlatzin had been totally crushed, and his Tepanec kingdom lay in ruins. The Aztec were now the greatest power in the Valley of Mexico and they set about rewriting history to glorify their past and depict themselves as the chosen people, the true heirs of the Toltec tradition. They burnt all the records of the conquered peoples, since these failed to mention the glorious Aztec past, and embarked on a vast programme of wars to

The *chinampas* or floating gardens near Mexico City—all that remains of the ancient Aztec waterways

expand their territory. For the first time since the downfall of the Toltec, there was a single great empire in Mexico.

By the sixteenth century the village of straw huts in the reeds had been transformed into a shining metropolis, Tenochtitlán, the capital of the huge Aztec empire. When the Spaniards entered the city at the end of 1519 they were astonished by what they saw. Bernal Díaz, one of the Spanish soldiers who accompanied Hernán Cortés, recorded his impressions:

We were struck with wonder and admiration at those big towers, the temples and buildings, all made of stone, rising from the water. Indeed some of us asked whether it was not all a dream.

We stood there looking. We saw the fresh water which came to supply the city and the bridges that were constructed at intervals on the causeways so that water could flow in and out from one part of the lake to another. We saw a great number of canoes, some coming with provisions and others returning with cargo and merchandise. We saw too that one could not pass from one house to another of the great city except over wooden drawbridges or by canoe.

They live almost as we do in Spain and with quite as much orderliness. It is wonderful to see how much sense they bring to the doing of everything. The noise and bustle of the market-place could be heard almost a league off and those who had been at Rome and Constantinople said that a market place so full of people, and so well and regularly attended, they had never

A reconstruction of Tenochtitlán, the Aztec capital, showing the main ceremonial precinct

beheld before. There were dealers in gold and silver and precious stones, feathers, cloth and embroidered goods. There were merchants who sold homespun clothing of cotton and others who sold cacao. There were people who sold a *henequen* cloth as well as rope and shoes made from the same plant, and its cooked roots which are sweet, all in a special section of the market set aside for them.

In another section they had jaguar skins, lions, deer and other animals some tanned and others not. Let us talk of the sellers of fruit and all the kinds of pottery made in a thousand shapes. I wonder why I waste these words in telling you what they sold in that great square, for I shall never finish describing everything in detail.

The city covered an area of about twenty square miles and had an estimated population of over 200,000, five times the size of the contemporary London of Henry VIII. A network of canals, bridges, causeways and raised earthworks were laid out with meticulous care. The bridges spanning the canals were, according to the Spaniards, so broad that ten horsemen could march abreast on them. The palaces, houses, market places and groups of temples were organised around two principal centres, Tenochtitlán and Tlatelolco.

The main square of Tenochtitlán was the focal point of the

city. It was the administrative and religious heart of the empire and the four main highways from the mainland led into it. Dominating the square was an immense temple-pyramid, rising to over 100 ft. On the top platform stood the shrines dedicated to the two main Aztec deities—Tlaloc, the rain god, who provided the water necessary for the cultivation of the soil, and Huitzilopochtli, the Aztec tribal god of war: on the one hand the religion of the settled peasant, on the other that of the warring nomad. There were said to be over seventy-two temples and buildings in the vast Temple Court, among them temples dedicated to Quetzalcoatl and Tezcatlipoca.

Near the great Temple-Pyramid was an enormous building which the Spaniards referred to as the 'Palace of Montezuma', although it was probably the seat of several branches of government. It was a maze of private courtyards, meeting chambers, granaries and storehouses. Accountants sat in offices continually at work compiling pictorial records of the tribute that arrived from all parts of the empire.

The city itself was divided into four sections known as 'calpullis' or wards. Each ward had its own temple and its own social and religious organisation. The simple lines of tribal democracy had been replaced by those of an aristocratic empire. At the head stood the Emperor, so high and splendid that ordinary people might not look upon him. At one time the Emperor shared his power with several high-ranking officials and when he died a council elected the new ruler, the man who was considered to be the most wise, capable and honourable. Gradually more and more personal power was invested in the Emperor, 'the one who speaks with authority', and his son or a close relative generally succeeded him.

By the time the Spaniards arrived, 'the one who speaks with authority' had become absolute ruler. The Emperor Montezuma, or Moctezuma which is a closer approximation to the pronunciation, lived a semi-divine existence surrounded by dazzling splendour. Everywhere he went he was borne on the shoulders of noblemen in a litter covered in gold and precious feathers. In his palace, a guard of 200 nobles lived in a room beside his own, only some of whom were permitted to speak to him. Those called to his presence had to go barefoot, wearing only the simplest of clothes. They went with their eyes cast down, for none were allowed to look at the Emperor, nor to turn their backs on him.

Montezuma lived in the palace with his councillors, his two wives and 'many other women as mistresses'. His court delighted in poetry, music and dancing. He was entertained by jugglers, tumblers and hump-backed dwarfs, as well as singers and dancers accompanied by flutes and drums. Hundreds of dishes were specially prepared for each meal, and when the Emperor began to eat he was shielded from onlookers by a screen richly decorated with gold.

The grounds of his palace were full of exotic plants and animals brought from the furthermost corners of the Empire. There were special gardens for every kind of animal, aviaries filled with hundreds of magnificantly coloured birds, and botanical gardens planted with sweet-scented shrubs, trees and flowering bushes. The Spaniards were clearly impressed: 'There was so much to see in these gardens, as everywhere else, that we could not tire of contemplating his riches and the large number of skilled Indians employed in the many crafts they practised.'

The ruling class was divided into two parallel hierarchies. On one side were those who administered and judged, and on the other were the priests, who by their faithful service in the temples caused the kindness of the gods to rain down upon earth. There were even separate courts of justice, one for noblemen and one for ordinary people. The chronicler Sahagún described the proceedings:

> All the complaints of the lower classes and common folk were heard by the judges in the court. Every day the common folk laid complaints before them. Calmly and prudently they heard the complaints and recorded them in their picture-book writing. The judges studied the complaints and, when they had tested their truth, they sought out and inquired of informers and witnesses, sized up the plaintiffs and what had been stolen and what was charged. Judges who unjustly discharged their office were seized and jailed.

On the whole administrators, priests and ruling dignitaries were drawn from the ranks of noblemen. In theory, numerous high positions were open to everyone, but in practice the humble son of a poor peasant had little chance of entering the group of the élite. The sons of noblemen had many advantages derived from the standing of their fathers, including a better education at special schools. Although they were not supposed to have any particular privileges and were meant to work as hard as anyone else in order to rise in the administrative or religious hierarchies, it was amongst these sons of lords that the Emperor found his judges, officials and priests. But if a nobleman did nothing outstanding in his lifetime, his children forfeited the right to any inherited distinction.

One group who were not part of the ruling class but who nevertheless enjoyed special privileges were the 'pochteca'. These were long-distance traders who obtained exotic products for the royal palace. The pochteca travelled hundreds of miles from the capital, often into foreign territory, where they gathered military intelligence as well as the needed merchandise for the Emperor. They rendered tribute to the palace in luxury goods and grew rich and powerful.

But the vast majority of the population were commoners who had little say in the running of the empire. They worked land which was owned collectively by their ward. An individual enjoyed the right to work a plot of land for his lifetime and could leave this right to his sons and heirs, but he could never own the land. If the plot remained unattended for over two years he forfeited his right to work it. Members of the ruling class lived in each ward and directed activities within the quarter, receiving a tribute of one third of all the produce grown by the commoners.

There was one way in which a commoner might climb to the élite—by becoming a successful warrior. The Aztec were primarily a warrior nation, an imperialist state steadily pursuing its aims of trade expansion by conquest. In a country perpetually at war the army offered brave and ambitious men a career that was particularly rich in honour and power. In Aztec society a man became wealthy because he was honoured; he was not honoured because he was wealthy. As a soldier distinguished himself, he rose in the hierarchy and earned the right to wear more and more splendid ornaments and costumes. He received gifts and tributes from various estates and was freed from farming his plot of land. Sometimes he was even given his own land, usually in a newly acquired territory, which was worked for him by the conquered peoples.

The Emperor promoted men to the higher ranks according to merit and often at the end of a battle a whole group would be promoted together. In this way the ruling class continually renewed itself, taking recruits from the general body of the

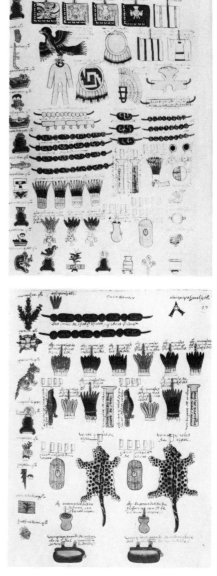

Aztec records from the Codex Mendoza showing the tribute levied from conquered peoples

Aztec stone carving showing the head of an Eagle Knight

people. In Tenochtitlán every man, whatever his origin, either was or wished to be a warrior, and boys were trained from an early age at special military schools. Successful warriors had an enviable and envied position. Their superiority was made evident not only by their clothes and rank but also by the privileged place they were given at all ceremonial occasions.

If a soldier did not do well in two or three successive campaigns, he had to give up the army and devote himself to his piece of land and his family. He would never be allowed to wear fine clothes or jewellery. If, however, he continued to acquit himself with honour he would eventually reach the upper category of men who participated in the distribution of revenue. Consistently successful warriors became members of the highest military order, the Knights of the Jaguar and Eagle. The Jaguar Knights were dedicated to the god of the night sky, the Eagle Knights to the god of the sun, for the eagle is a creature of the sun that, like the sun, floats through the sky. When they went into battle the Eagle Knights wore tunics of feathers and

Aztec warriors of the highest military orders, the Knights of the Jaguar and the Eagle, from the codex compiled by Fray Bernardino de Sahagún

headdresses in the form of an eagle's head, with its beak over their forehead. The Jaguar Knights wore tunics made of jaguar skins.

At its height, the Aztec Empire stretched over 500 miles, from the Gulf Coast to the Pacific, while its trade routes and military campaigns reached far into the south. It was an empire made up of a loose federation of conquered peoples, all of whom were forced to pay tribute to their conquerors. Thousands of tons of maize and beans, millions of cotton cloaks, war costumes, shields and feather head dresses and all kinds of luxury goods poured into the capital. Meticulous lists were drawn up stipulating exactly what each conquered province must provide, in what quantities, and how often. As long as the tribute was paid in full and promptly, the people were normally left alone. No attempt was made to force them to adopt the Aztec way of life or to learn the Nahuatl language—in fact the rulers of Tenochtitlán held the tributary peoples in contempt. If, on the other hand, a city or province tried to regain its former independence and refused to pay tribute, a military expedition was sent in to restore order and punish the rebels.

The Aztec's prime motive for war, however, was not to gain more territory or to receive tribute, but to obtain live captives for sacrifice. They believed their survival depended on providing the gods with a constant supply of hearts taken from captive warriors, and that meant perpetual war. They even engaged with their neighbours in what were called 'Flower Wars', in which the whole object of both sides was to gain captives. The success of a warrior was not measured by how many men he killed but by how many he brought back alive. Of the gods who could only be propitiated by human sacrifice Coatlícue, the earth goddess who wore the mask of death, was particularly greedy and pitiless. Every night she devoured the sun and every morning gave it rebirth. To the Aztec there was always the fear that the sun might set and never rise again, and darkness would overwhelm the world for ever. Only that precious liquid, human blood, could avert such a catastrophe. It was said that at the inauguration of the great temple-pyramid of Tenochtitlán, over 20,000 prisoners were sacrificed, in what was for the Aztec a sacred duty towards the sun, a necessity for the welfare of man.

The Spaniards were horrified by the scenes they witnessed in the temples, where priests dressed in black robes, their hair

Codex, annotated by the Spaniards, showing warriors with their captives

Left Colossal statue of Coatlícue, the Old Goddess of the Earth and patron of life and death. Two serpents rise from the neck, meeting to form a face. She wears a necklace of human hearts and hands with a pendant skull, while her skirt is made of writhing snakes.

Right Quetzalcoatl, the Plumed Serpent, thought by the Aztec to be the inventor of all great things such as writing, painting and the calendar

Aztec sacrificial knife, with a mosaic-
encrusted handle representing an
Eagle Warrior

matted with blood, presided over the ceremonies. Bernal Díaz
left this account:

> They strike open the wretched Indian's chest with flint knives
> and hastily tear out the palpitating heart, which with the blood
> they present to the idols in whose name they have performed the
> sacrifice. The head they hang up on a beam and the body of the
> sacrificed man is not eaten but given to the beasts of prey. . .
>
> All the walls of the shrines were so splashed and caked with
> blood that they and the floor too were black. The whole place
> stank abominably. . .
>
> Cortés, said to the Emperor Montezuma through our
> interpreters, 'Lord Montezuma I cannot imagine how a prince as
> great and wise as your Majesty can have failed to realise that
> these idols of yours are not gods but evil things, the proper name
> for which is devils.' Montezuma replied, angered. 'Lord
> Malinche, I should not have shown you my gods. We hold them
> to be very good. They give us health and rain and crops and
> weather, and all the victories we desire. So we are bound to
> worship them and sacrifice to them and I beg you to say nothing
> more against them. . . . We have worshipped our own gods from
> the beginning and know them to be good. No doubt yours are
> good also, but do not trouble to tell us any more about them. . .

Offerings of blood for the gods, from an
Aztec codex

Perhaps every culture has its own idea of cruelty. The
Spaniards, so genuinely upset by the scenes of human sacrifice,
nevertheless committed the most horrifying tortures themselves, mutilating and massacring in the name of their god. The
Aztec, unperturbed by the rituals in their blood-soaked temples,
were appalled by the tortures brought from the land of the
Inquisition. To the Aztec human sacrifice was neither cruel nor
horrifying, it was simply necessary to save the world.

Religion regulated the life of every single Aztec. Public and
private life, and each stage of a person's progress from birth to
death was dictated by the will of the gods. Each day had good or
evil portents according to the interpretation of the priests, for

the Aztec were obsessed with auspicious days and paid the greatest attention to signs and omens, compiling painted manuscripts dealing with mythology, ritual, divination and history. They saw themselves as the chosen people, the favourites of the gods. According to one version of their history, the Pyramids of Teotihuacán were built by the gods when the world began and the sun and moon were created. The arts of writing and painting, the invention of the calendar and all great things were the creation of the Toltec and their god Quetzalcoatl—the fair-skinned Quetzalcoatl, who was driven out by the evil Teźcaltipoca, but who would one day return. 'In truth Quetzalcoatl is alive', people said. 'He is not dead. He is to return. He will come to rule over these lands again.' For generations this prophecy had haunted the Aztec rulers.

The date of the return of Quetzalcoatl had been predicted for a particular day in spring that occurred once every fifty-two years. One such year in European notation was 1519. As the year approached, the Emperor Montezuma became aware of strange signs and portents: a comet appeared in the sky like a

Basalt mask showing the flayed skin from the face of a victim sacrificed to the god Xipe Totec

The Sun Stone or Aztec 'calendar', with glyphs marking days, months and cosmic cycles

'tongue of fire'; high up on the Great Pyramid, a fire broke out in the temple of Huitzilopochtli; monstrous births, some with two heads, were reported. As the ominous signs continued, Montezuma became anxious and depressed. One day messengers returned from the coast to tell the Emperor that great mountains had been seen moving on the waters. When news of the landing of the fair-skinned, bearded Cortés came to Montezuma, he was convinced that Quetzalcoatl had indeed returned.

The Aztec Empire began to fall apart as soon as the Spaniards landed. Many of the subjugated peoples were only too pleased to take the Spanish side against their oppressors. The small band of Spanish soldiers, with their horses and cannon, marched victoriously up into the highlands. The Emperor Montezuma, feeling powerless in the face of the will of the gods, welcomed them into his city. His speech was recorded by Bernal Díaz.

> I have been holding the throne for you. I have been governing the kingdom that the divine Quetzalcoatl abandoned. Upon this seat I have sat unworthily, reigning over your vassals. Now the written prophecies and traditions of my ancestors have come true. . . . So rest and be at peace, for we welcome you back and are overjoyed at your return.

Montezuma allowed himself to be taken prisoner without resistance. But his people did not surrender so easily. They took up arms against the Spaniards and eventually forced them to flee the capital. In the retreat which followed, two-thirds of the Spanish force were either drowned in the lake, slaughtered or captured. During the battle, the Emperor Montezuma, a prisoner in Spanish quarters, was killed perhaps by the Spaniards or perhaps by his own people, who felt he had betrayed them.

Montezuma's brother, Cuitlahuac, took over as ruler, but within six months he was dead of smallpox, a disease brought by the Spaniards. Cuauhtemoc, a young warrior, was given command. He realised that the Spaniards were not gods but enemies bent on the destruction of the empire, but that realisation was already too late. Tenochtitlán had gradually been cut off from its tributary provinces and food was running out. The siege lasted eighty days, with Cortés pressing closer and closer, moving in by land and water while the people starved. On Wednesday, 13 August 1521, the brave Cuauh-

yeqtla ti tetzavitl yn mal ques.

Spanish *Conquistadores* attacking
Tenochtitlán, from the codex known as
the Lienzo de Tlaxcala

temoc finally surrendered his beleagured city. An anonymous
poem in Nahuatl tells what followed:

> Our spears lie broken in the streets,
> Our hair is torn
> Gone are the roofs of our houses
> Their walls red with blood
> Worms crawl across the streets and squares
> Brains cling to the walls
> Red are the waters
> Lurid as tan bark
> And when we drink the water tastes of fear.

After 1521 the whole structure, religious and social, that
had centred on Tenochtitlán collapsed utterly. All that has
survived of pre-Hispanic culture is the inheritance of the
ordinary Indian peasant who, with his hut, his plot of land and
his turkeys, was of little interest to the chroniclers of either
civilisation.

Today there are some 880,000 Indians who still speak the
Aztec language of Nahuatl. They are the largest indigenous

group in Mexico but, scattered throughout the country, they do not form a political unit, nation or tribe. The main element which unites them is their language, Nahuatl, whose many dialects are all mutually intelligible. After 450 years of co-existence with Spanish, it has undergone considerable change: much of the ancient religious and political vocabulary and the elaborate literary forms have been lost, and a number of modern words have found their way into daily speech. But fundamentally it is still the same language that the Aztec spoke.

The Nahua Indians have an economy largely based on maize, which they cultivate much as the Aztec did. The seeds are sown using a 'digging stick' with which holes are made a few feet apart. Three or four grains of maize are placed in each hole together with a bean, so that when the shoots appear the bean is trained round the maize stalks. As in ancient times, a successful harvest is crucial to their livelihood. Although the Nahua all profess Christianity, religious rites are still, as

Nahua family from Zoatecpan in the Puebla Highlands, where Nahuatl is still widely spoken

elsewhere in Mexico, closely connected with the blessing of the crops and the cycle of the seasons which derive from pre-Christian times. In some villages there are old men who are expert 'rain petitioners' or 'those who prevent the hail'. Bread, fruit and other delicacies are sometimes left in caves as offerings to God and the saints.

Most religious ceremonies are now held on the feast days of Roman Catholic saints, but special dances are still an integral part of all rituals. To the Indian, dance is no mere pastime, but an act of deep religious significance. Failure to perform the ritual dances may bring calamity to the community. But if God and the Saints are pleased, the village will be blessed with good crops and a thriving livestock. The role of the dancer is considered so holy and important that he must be purified before he can take part.

Every year at the Feast of St Francis the ancient Quetzal dance is performed by the Nahua Indians in the small mountain town of Cuetzalan. In Aztec times this ceremony was probably connected with agriculture and astronomy; now too it is performed to ensure a successful harvest—and also to honour the saint. On the day of the feast the courtyard in front of the church is packed with people who have come from all the surrounding villages. Many of the women wear their traditional costumes, piling their hair high with skeins of purple wool which was a feature of pre-Hispanic dress. Bobbing above the crowds are the extraordinary head-dresses of the Quetzal dancers, immense circular frameworks of reeds interlaced with multicoloured paper and strips of ribbon. Each huge coloured wheel is attached to a small conical cap which is tied onto the dancer's head. Small feathers on the tips of the spokes are the only reminders that once the whole head-dress was made of the glorious iridescent plumes of the Quetzal bird. For the rest the dancers wear bright red trousers and a red top, all fringed with yellow, and in either hand they carry a gourd rattle and brightly coloured handkerchief. Each dancer makes and pays for his own costume with the help of his family.

Before the performance begins, the dancers visit the church to offer prayers and seek the blessing of the saint. Then they return to the courtyard where, accompanied by a musician playing simultaneously on a reed flute and small drum, they begin their strange and ancient ritual. Each dancer marks out the four cardinal points of the compass with his right foot, then

Traditional Nahua costumes from Cuetzalan, Puebla. The hair is piled high with skeins of purple wool (*see colour plate 32*)

The Quetzal Dance, still performed by the Nahua Indians of Puebla, but now in honour of the Christian saints (*see also colour plate 33*)

stamps and rotates to symbolise the passage of time and the cycle of the seasons. Their timing is so precise that all the vast coloured head-dresses twirl backwards and forwards in unison. The dance continues on and off for many hours, and the weight of the head-dresses reduces nearly all the dancers to complete exhaustion.

Perhaps in these dances we get a distant glimpse of the Aztec past, of the sumptuous world of warriors and nobles with their dazzling head-dresses and brilliantly coloured feather cloaks. But of the great Aztec temples and cities little remains, for the Spaniards smashed almost everything to the ground. Within a few years of the Aztec surrender, they had stripped the country of its treasures, destroyed it as a civilisation and reduced its people to the level of serfs. A few placid lagoons are all that survive of the beautiful 'floating' city of Tenochtitlán. On the ruins of the great Aztec capital now stands modern Mexico City.

There is an irony in the fact that today, just over 400 years after the destruction of Tenochtitlán, parts of Mexico City are being pulled down to allow for the restoration of the main Aztec temple, the great Pyramid dedicated to Huitzilopochtli and Tlaloc. The project began in 1978 when an Aztec ceremonial stone was discovered in an area known to be the site of the great temple. The stone is carved with a rather macabre display of dismembered limbs, representing Coyolxauhqui, the goddess of

Left Aztec ceremonial stone representing Coyolxauhqui, Goddess of the Moon, recently excavated in Mexico City

Above The Moon Goddess, Coyolxauhqui

the moon, who was cut up into little pieces by her brother Huitzilopochtli for the attempted murder of their mother, the terrifying Coatlicue, goddess of the earth. The stone is a major monument of Aztec civilisation, so important a find that the authorities were prompted to give archaeologists permission to excavate the whole site, whose location had never been in

Stone serpents at the foot of the Aztec temple-pyramid at Tenayuca

doubt, but where they now hope to uncover more exciting remains.

Outside Mexico City more of the Aztec heritage has survived, in a few smaller temples like those of Tenayuca and Santa Cecilia; and at Malinalco, high in the mountains seventy miles from the capital, a small temple contains sculptures carved out of bedrock and representing the jaguars and eagles that were the emblems of the two Aztec warrior orders. Together these provide some context for the awe-inspiring monumental sculpture of the Aztec that crams the Museum of Anthropology in Mexico City. But perhaps it is in their poetry that we come closest to the real Aztec, a people haunted by death and the ephemeral nature of things.

The Aztec pyramid at Santa Cecilia, with its temple still intact

Let no one be overwhelmed by sadness
Let no one's thoughts wander about over the earth.
Here are our precious flowers and songs.
May our friends delight in them.
May the sadness fade out of our hearts.

Oh friends, this earth is only lent to us.
We shall have to leave our fine poems,
We shall have to leave our beautiful flowers.
That is why I am sad as I sing for the sun,
We shall have to leave our fine poems,
We shall have to leave our beautiful flowers.

*   *   *

Shall my heart go
As flowers that wither?
Some day shall my name be nothing?
My fame nothing, anywhere upon the earth?
At least let us have flowers; at least
let us have singing.
How shall my heart manage
We go about on the earth in vain.

* * *

Where shall I go
Where shall I go
The road of the dual god.
Is by chance your house the place of the dead?
Is it, by chance, the interior of heaven? Or is earth the only
place for those who are killed or sacrificed.

* * *

Does one really live upon the earth?
Not for ever on the earth, only for a short time here.
Even jade shatters,
Even gold breaks,
Even Quetzal plumes tear,
Not for ever on the earth, only a short time here.

* * *

3 The People of the Valley

The State of Oaxaca lies in the south of Mexico, at the meeting-point of the two great mountain ranges that border the Atlantic and the Pacific. It joins with the states of Guerrero and Puebla to the west and to the north, and with the states of Veracruz and Chiapas to the east and south. Constantly shaken by earthquakes, it is a region of mountain peaks and narrow valleys. Near the centre of the state three large valleys converge, forming what is known as the Valley of Oaxaca. A warm yet gentle climate and a good rainfall make this the most fertile region of the state, and archaeologists believe that man has lived here since the very earliest times. It seems likely that the domestication of edible plants began in this area, and that maize has been cultivated here for over 6000 years.

Today Oaxaca remains a predominantly Indian state with a larger indigenous population than almost any other region of Mexico. A census taken in 1960 gave the total number of inhabitants as 1,727,266 with an Indian population of 683,818. But the term 'Indian' was used only to cover speakers of Indian languages, so it would probably be true to say that over seventy-five per cent of the inhabitants of Oaxaca count as

Trique family from the Highlands of the Mixteca wearing traditional everyday dress (*see also colour plate 4*)

87

General view of the ceremonial centre of Monte Albán, built high in the hills of Oaxaca. Its origins stretch back to *c.* 700 BC (*see also colour plate 15*)

Indian, in that they follow a pattern of life that has changed little since the Conquest.

Several Indian groups inhabit the southern highlands of Mexico, such as the Mixe, the Chinantec, the Trique, the Popoloca or the Cuicatec, and the differences in language and tradition which persist today were present long before the Spanish invasion. But the two Oaxacan races to have played the most decisive role in the development of Mexican civilisation are the Zapotec and the Mixtec, whose achievements equalled those of the Aztec in the centre of Mexico or the Maya to the south. Today the descendants of these great peoples occupy the same territory, and speak the same languages as their ancestors, many of whose traditions and beliefs they carry on.

Archaeological evidence suggests that the first civilisation to emerge in the Valley of Oaxaca was linked with the Olmec culture of the Gulf Coast. Around 900 BC the Olmec art style had begun to spread across Mexico and by about 700 BC their influence seems to have reached Oaxaca. High on a hill top, surrounded by magnificent scenery, in a site known today as Monte Albán, evidence of that influence can be seen.

This consists of stone slabs, originally used to form a frieze around the base of a temple. They portray strange tumbling

Above and left Stone slabs from Monte Albán with carved figures which have become known as 'The Dancers'. Dating from around 700 BC, they show a strong Olmec influence

figures which have become known as 'The Dancers'. What they signify has given rise to endless speculation. They are shown in a diversity of postures, which has been variously interpreted as representing dancers and tumblers, bisected corpses—their internal organs revealed—and patients undergoing complex operations. The scrolls and flowers which emerge from the genitals have been taken as symbols of water and wind, to suggest regeneration and the cycle of life. However the closed eyes, the sexual mutilation and the wildly disposed limbs are rather those of dead captives, and their nakedness too points to the common Middle American custom of stripping clothes and ornaments from the dead foe.

Sometimes glyphs are shown either on or beside the figures, which may be the name glyph either of the person or of the place he came from. These indicate that this early people must have been among the first in Mexico to use a writing system; and an inscribed stela suggests the early use of a calendrical system. The figures are carved in a style which seems to derive from that of the Olmec, although it lacks the refinement of Olmec originals. The heavy, downturned mouths do certainly suggest an Olmec influence, but beyond this the culture remains a mystery. How its society was ordered, and who its gods were, is still not known.

By 300 BC the building at Monte Albán of new structures in a different style suggests the arrival of another people, possibly invaders. By them, too, panels not unlike those portraying the Dancers were used for decoration. The most interesting building from this period has a strange spear-like shape which suggests that it served as an observatory for the study of the

Monte Albán: the structure in the foreground dates from 300 BC and may have been used as an observatory

stars. A number of the Dancer slabs were re-used in the facing, but others carved at the time bear inscriptions which may denote places. At the foot of each are inverted heads, possibly as a symbol of conquest.

It was during this time that funerary architecture began to develop. Whereas the founders of Monte Albán had been content to bury their dead in simple, rectangular, box-shaped tombs of stone set into the hillside, their successors constructed stone stairways leading down to underground vaulted chambers with small niches in the side and back walls. Here the dead were laid out with offerings, presumably in readiness for the long journey that lay ahead of them. In one of these tombs an extraordinary jade mask, thought by many to be of Olmec workmanship, was recently found. Made from twenty-five pieces of jade, with eyes and teeth of white shell, it represents the Bat God, a deity associated by succeeding cultures with darkness and death.

Whoever these early peoples may have been, by the third or Classic stage at Monte Albán the inhabitants were Zapotec. Incorporating earlier structures and superimposing their own, they gradually built up a ceremonial centre covering an area of about fifteen sq miles which included a ball court, temples, tombs, observatories and houses for the ruling and priestly classes.

Little is known of the origins of the Zapotec people. It seems likely that their homeland lay farther to the north and east, and that they arrived in the Valley of Oaxaca at some time before the Christian era. The exceptionally fertile plains surrounding Monte Albán, watered by the Atoyac river, and the semi-tropical climate made this an attractive place to settle in. It is generally assumed that they drove out the people that had preceded them. By AD 500 the Zapotec had become the first truly distinctive culture to evolve in the area, and their rule was to last for another 400 years.

The overall effect which they achieved at Monte Albán is one of great harmony. The vast central plaza, enclosed by platforms and pyramids, is 1000 ft long and gives a feeling of spaciousness and light. To the north a great stairway, believed to be the widest in the Americas, leads to a platform bearing the remains of two rows of circular columns. Adjoining the northeast corner of the great plaza lies the ball court with its sloping walls where religious festivals, games and rituals took place.

Jade mask from Monte Albán, possibly of Olmec workmanship, showing a bat god

Pyramids and temples were faced with stucco and brightly painted.

Even now, more than four and a half centuries after the Conquest, many Zapotec regard Monte Albán with awe and pride. Some even believe that caves in the hillsides near Monte Albán were the original homes of their ancestors, and in recent times offerings have been left for the ancient gods.

Today the Zapotec form the largest indigenous group in Oaxaca, and number over 300,000. Many are still unable to speak Spanish, and the Zapotec language itself has many

Reconstruction of Monte Albán during its height as a Zapotec ceremonial centre, *c.* AD 500

variations. Most are village farmers and live scattered throughout central and southern Oaxaca, linked by an extensive trade network that has been built up over the centuries, and centres on the market-place.

One of the largest and most popular Indian markets in the state is held in the town of Tlacolula, little more than eighteen miles south of Oaxaca City. Throughout the week the vast paved square near the Colonial church is virtually deserted. On Sundays it is transformed. Before the sun has risen, approaching roads are full of horse-drawn carts and local buses crowded with passengers and their merchandise, including live chickens and sacks of chili peppers, while the roofs are piled high with

Potter on his way to market, with his load
wrapped in rush mats

bales and bundles. Many people travel on foot with heavy
loads of fruit and vegetables or pots precariously balanced
on their backs and supported by a tumpline, or cord, across the
forehead.

In the faint light of dawn, the traders take up their
accustomed positions in the square. By the fountain, flower-
sellers lay out their lilies, roses or marigolds. Other women,
wrapped in shawls to keep out the early-morning chill, arrange
their onions, peppers and tomatoes in tidy heaps on the ground,
or watch over great baskets of hot *tortillas*, freshly-made that
morning, and clay cauldrons of frothy chocolate or steaming
coffee, sweetened with brown sugar. On the outskirts of the

The People of the Valley 93

Making *tortillas* or maize 'pancakes' in a Zapotec village

square, the men are meanwhile erecting stalls and trestle tables, using long wooden poles and white canvas awnings. Merchandise is divided up by areas. Drip-glazed pots are heaped up in one section; palm mats, baskets and hats in another.

By seven o'clock the market is already in full swing, with customers examining the goods and haggling over prices in the Zapotec language as often as in Spanish. Those who come to buy or sell have often travelled long distances—there are Zapotec from the mountains, as well as Indians from other groups. For most visitors, this is the high point of the week. Children look in wonder at the crowds and the abundance of merchandise, while their parents examine blankets for the quality of the weave, look over the pigs and poultry in the livestock section, or discuss an ailment with one of the herbalists who may prescribe an infusion made from tree-bark or the wearing of a lucky amulet. As evening approaches, traders become increasingly anxious to dispose of their goods. Prices drop, and many items are finally bartered away. By seven o'clock the square is empty once again, and will remain so until the following Sunday.

Although the Zapotec are today dispersed over a large area, they keep a strong sense of identity, choosing to live in close-knit communities where the old traditions can be maintained. Not far from Tlacolula and its weekly market, is the village of San Martín Tilcajete with its old Colonial church, damaged over the centuries by successive earthquakes, and about three hundred one-roomed houses. Interspersed with plots of land, these are reached by dirt tracks marked with the imprint of wooden cartwheels and the hooves of oxen. Outside the village lie the fields, sown as in other parts of the Valley with maize, squash and beans, and also a stretch of common land from which wood for fires or carpentry may be freely taken. Indeed it is as a wood-working community that San Martín is known throughout the region. The tradition goes back a long way; and many families give pride of place in their homes to ornately carved benches and other pieces of furniture dating from the Colonial era.

Celestino Cruz is a woodcarver, who is proud of his Indian origin and the customs of San Martín. He lives with his wife, Paula, and their four children in a windowless one-room house of bricks on a hill overlooking the village and the surrounding countryside. His yard, with its barn for storing grain in one corner and a cooking area in the other, is full of wood waiting to be carved, of farming implements and chickens. Helped by her small daughter, Paula does as many as possible of her household tasks outside in the open air: mending the family's clothes, or de-husking maize from their fields and grinding it to make *tamales*, the drink known as '*atole*', or the *tortillas* that accompany every meal.

When Celestino is at home, he does his woodcarving in the yard, sitting on a low stool. Masks are an important feature of his work, and he explains why: 'During the Carnival, all the villagers come out wearing the best masks they can get, and dressed in disguise for fun. Masks were much used in the past, too.' Celestino paints the masks he makes in bright colours, and they may portray jaguars, men and women, or death's heads, according to his inspiration. He also likes to experiment with other types of carvings:

> I don't only make masks. I've actually been through a lot of different phases. I've carved Christs, horses, nativity scenes, miniature carts and a number of other things. More recently I've been doing some quite complicated pieces with devils and skeletons. I don't want to dedicate myself to just one thing, but would much rather draw on my imagination when I work.

Despite Celestino's obvious pride in his own creative ability, he retains a deep admiration for the skill of his forefathers:

> Right up until the present day, I and many other artisans have continued to preserve the traditions of Oaxaca. And I hope that

many of us will continue for a long time to make pieces like the ones our ancestors left behind them. Of course it isn't possible to make them identical—that just can't be done. But one can at least continue to use a number of their designs, and that's also important.

Attached though Celestino is to Oaxaca and to his village, he has found that he cannot earn enough as a farmer and woodcarver to support his family:

Here in San Martín, the majority are craftsmen, and they work in much the same way that I do. But the fact is, I just can't afford to stay here. Instead I've been obliged to go to Mexico City where I work in a shop run by FONART, the government organisation which promotes crafts. There are lots of wooden pieces on sale there, many of which have been carved by us, the villagers of San Martín.

He is not the only one who has been forced to leave home. A number of his friends also work in the city, returning as he does for fleeting visits and to plant their fields, which will be cared for in their absence by close relatives. As Celestino dusts the merchandise in the shop or walks the city streets, his family and his village are never far from his thoughts. The dirt paths that he once took on his way to school are now being taken by his children, who send him drawings and letters with friends returning to the city. Many have travelled even further than Celestino, however, chancing their luck as labourers, farmers or construction workers in the United States.

Although the Zapotec language has almost died out in San Martín, the inhabitants feel very close to their ancestors who lived in the Valley so long before them, and Celestino expresses his feelings like this:

For my part, I feel really satisfied and very happy that my forefathers thought in the way they did, and were as they were. There have been many changes, and people today are more learned than they used to be, but I think that life is much the same for us as it was for our ancestors. We feel the same longing to be happy that they felt, and we continue in the same way. We feel glad and peaceful to be living this life, and I think we shouldn't undervalue what our forefathers left for us. Monte Albán is a very special and important place. It is my belief that if they hadn't left us what they did, Oaxaca today would be a ruined state.

Celestino Cruz carving a mask in his village, San Martín Tilcajete

Zapotec funerary urn of grey pottery: Cocijo, the Rain God

Conceived by the ancient Zapotec as a ceremonial centre in honour of their gods, Monte Albán was also a great necropolis where dead rulers and priests were buried in long rows of tombs that bordered the central plaza. Over 200 of these often ornate tombs have been excavated, and a large number of funerary objects and offerings have been discovered, including ceramic burial urns showing gods or priests wearing god-masks.

The Zapotec gods, as was natural for an agricultural people, represented the forces of nature. The most important was a Rain God, Cocijo, who was identified by the scrolls round his eyes and by his serpent tongue, forked to symbolise lightning. Xipe Totec was the God of Spring. Also known as the Flayed

Above Zapotec funerary urn of grey pottery: Xipe Totec, the God of Spring

Right Zapotec funerary urn set in the wall of a tomb at Monte Albán

One, he was portrayed wearing a human skin to represent the new vegetation that covers the earth each year. The youthful God of Maize had a corn plant as his special attribute. No less often shown was the Bat God. Previously honoured by other races, he was envisaged by the Zapotec as a squat figure with an elaborate head-dress and shoulder ornaments to denote spread wings.

The funerary urns that were placed in tombs to honour these deities represented them as seated, cross-legged figures, entirely covering the front of the pot. Great attention was paid to head-dresses and ornaments, and coloured paints were often used for decoration. Although the Zapotec later began to produce urns in large numbers from moulds, earlier methods consisted in

Seated, cross-legged god covering the front of a Zapotec funerary urn

modelling the figures by hand, cutting out details with a knife while the clay was still damp.

Centuries have passed, but the Zapotec have never lost their skill as potters. Many communities in the Valley supplement their income by producing water jars, clay griddles and other items to sell at local markets and fairs. San Bartolo Coyotepec has a long tradition as a potting village, and its celebrated blackware is much sought after. Juan and Reina Galan are brother and sister, and they live with their family on the outskirts of the village. Theirs is a windowless, one-room house of bricks which faces the open countryside and the mountains beyond. Goats, cows and a donkey crop the grass that grows in the large untidy patio, and turkeys peck for food among the

The People of the Valley 99

Reina Galan, from the village of San Bartolo Coyotepec, making a pot on the traditional 'Zapotec wheel' — two upturned dishes

sherds and discarded pots that surround the kiln.

Pots are fired on average once a week, and Reina spends the intervening days working on a new batch. While Juan is out in the fields, she sits by the house in the shade of the porch, kneading and forming the local clay, by pushing her fist into a ball of moist clay and hollowing it out. To help her with the next stage, Reina uses an ancient device known as the 'Zapotec wheel' consisting of two dishes, one of which supports the pot while it rotates upon the second. As it spins Reina builds up the walls of the pot by adding coils of clay. Surfaces are smoothed as she progresses, and eventually the pot is given a flaring lip with the help of a piece of damp leather. Once finished, the pottery is left to dry, then scraped with a strip of tin for perfect smoothness, and finally polished with a stone. Helped by a niece or younger sister, she often scratches decorative motifs onto the clay with a sharp nail.

When the day arrives for the pots to be fired, they are set out in the sunshine to warm up. Ancient in design, the kilns used in San Bartolo Coyotepec are now found nowhere else in Mexico. The brick-lined firing chamber lies below ground, and only the round opening is immediately visible. A pit, dug alongside, allows the potter to climb down and feed the furnace, which is underneath the kiln. When Juan has lit the fire, he accommodates the pots in the kiln, piling them up one by one as they are handed to him by the women and children. This is a family

Reina Galan and family sealing off the underground kiln with potsherds and mud

event, and everyone joins in. Once the pottery is in position and the heat of the wood fire has begun to rise, the kiln is covered over with potsherds and later completely sealed off with mud.

Pottery is usually left overnight and the fire, choked by lack of oxygen, gives off clouds of smoke and soot which impregnate the clay. Early next morning Juan uncovers the kiln and removes the blackened pots. This is done before the sun has fully risen, lest its heat rekindle the fire. When Reina's polishing rag has removed the grime, surfaces gleam with a metallic brilliance, and it is this black sheen which makes the jars, jugs, dishes and toy whistles of San Bartolo Coyotepec unique throughout Mexico.

Potting is an uncertain and risky occupation. Should the temperature rise too high during firing the pots might lose their blackness or even crack. Should the temperature remain too low the pots would be too fragile for use. But Reina and Juan, like the other potters in their community, seem to have an instinctive understanding of their craft, based on their years of experience. Asked how she learnt to make pots, Reina replied:

> From my parents. I can remember playing with the clay as a child, but then after that, as I grew older, I began to work it more, to work it better.'

But Reina also realises that hers is a skill inherited from countless generations of Zapotec:

I can hardly remember anything about my ancestors. But I do know that my forefathers found fragments of what had been made before, and that's how they began to do the same. And then, after that, we grew up and we were taught to work in the same way that they did.'

During the time that Reina's ancestors were part of the great civilisation at Monte Albán, countless craftsmen, architects, artists and builders put their creativity at the service of the gods, raising temples and pyramids and filling the tombs with a wealth of burial offerings. But then, around AD 900, the Zapotec abandoned their ceremonial city. Quite why, no one knows, but it seems likely that their desertion was linked with the arrival in the Valley of another people: the warlike Mixtec.

Although their origins are lost in time, the Mixtec lived during the sixth and seventh centuries AD in the areas that correspond today to northern Oaxaca and southern Puebla. Some of the best pre-Hispanic manuscripts to have survived are of Mixtec origin, and from the interpretations given so far

Details from the Mixtec codex known as the Zouche-Nuttall. This sequence has been interpreted as follows: (a Lady Three-Flint meeting her future husband Lord Five-Flower; (b The happy couple shown having a ritual bath and in the marriage bed; (c Lady Three-Flint bathing with a snail, the symbol of maternity; (d the birth of her child.

scholars have been able to get some idea of the history of this people. Painted onto strips of deerskin, which are folded concertina fashion, a series of brightly-coloured pictograms recount genealogies and historic events, as well as calendrical and religious themes. Innumerable human figures remain frozen in time against a whitened background. Shown in profile according to the conventions of the period, warriors advance to do battle, devout men and women bring offerings to the temple, kings display elaborate costumes of woven cloth and skins ornamented with feathers, while a naked priest tears out a victim's heart. Not all the books chronicle great conquests or martial events: some portray royal weddings and the birth of children.

The saga of the warrior-king Eight-Deer (also known as Tiger-Claw) has been pieced together from several manuscripts. He succeeded first in welding the Mixtec into a single nation, and then in annexing other neighbouring groups, through battle and also through diplomatic intermarriage with the

c

d

The People of the Valley 103

daughters of powerful chieftains. Polygamy must have been common Mixtec practice among the nobility, for Eight-Deer gained four if not five wives in this way, and considerably extended his dominions. One hundred years after his death, according to the interpretations made by some scholars, a conquering army of Mixtec warriors moved into the central valley of Oaxaca, subduing settlements along the way. A diplomatic marriage ensured an uneasy peace with the Zapotec, and the newcomers settled in the area.

By the eleventh century the Mixtec had achieved a distinctive culture, re-using many of the old Zapotec settlements and establishing a number of their own. The finest of these, at Mitla, included five main groups of buildings, some of which were perhaps the homes of chiefs or priests, while others were used for ceremonial purposes. Rooms were long and low, with elongated panels of high-relief stone mosaics on the walls. Although most were decorated with these geometrical motifs composed of countless stone elements, one or two rooms had

The Mixtec ceremonial centre at Mitla *c.* AD 800 (*see also page 12*)

wall-paintings above the doorways in a style reminiscent of the picture-books.

Pottery was another field in which the ancient Mixtec showed great skill, and other sites such as Zaachila have yielded up many splendid examples. One pot discovered there has a humming bird perched on the rim, and features exquisitely-painted motifs in various colours. These include symbols, angular patterns and portrayals of the gods.

But it was as metal-smiths and lapidaries that the Mixtec excelled. Their best work was unequalled throughout Mexico, though little of their precious metal-working has survived. When the Spanish Conquistadores took over Mexico early in the sixteenth century, they melted down the Indian treasures into bullion and a royal decree was issued forbidding the native craftsmen to possess or even work the precious metals of their land. Then in 1932, excavations at Monte Albán led to an amazing discovery. Many of the tombs of this basically Zapotec site had been re-used by the Mixtec for the burial of their own priests and rulers. The Mexican archaeologist, Alfonso Caso, led the explorations. In the course of his excavation he came upon a subterranean tomb, into which he peered through a narrow aperture lit by a flashlight. An astonishing sight met his eyes:

Mixtec polychrome pot with a hummingbird on the rim (height $2\frac{3}{4}$ inches)

Detail showing the stone mosaics that decorate many of the walls at Mitla.

The People of the Valley 105

The first thing to be seen upon entering the tomb was a great white vessel in the centre of the second chamber. Upon illuminating it from the inside, I saw that it was translucent. The material of this beautiful amphora is a variety of onyx marble known in Mexico as 'tecali'. On the threshold, or vestibule, separating the two chambers of the tomb, and in the centre of a great pile of bones, objects of gold glittered—beads, little bells and so on. Strung on the arm bones of one of the skeletons were ten bracelets, six of gold and four of silver. I found here also what at first appeared to be a tiny vessel of hammered gold, ornamented with the figure of a spider, but which subsequently I have come to think was used as a clasp for a belt.

Finally, near the door of the tomb, I saw a golden diadem and next to it the plume, twisted and bent, which at one time served to decorate it. Upon turning to leave, I was attracted by the skull, decorated with a mosaic of turquoise, which was in the first chamber near the threshold. . . . Upon lighting the floor of the tomb, we found it aglow with pearls, golden beads and innumerable small, flat pieces of turquoise that at one time had composed a rich mosaic. It was impossible to reconstruct it, notwithstanding the fact that my first care was to see if I could save it, even if only in part.

As we left the tomb, I realised the incalculable richness of my discovery from a material, an artistic and a scientific viewpoint. I had no knowledge of any previous discovery in America of such a treasure.

Buried in a sitting position, the nine corpses accompanied by all this funerary wealth had become mere piles of bones over the centuries, while the dampness of the tomb had caused perishable materials such as wood and cloth to rot. But more than 500 objects have survived. These include the *tecali* goblet admired by Caso, and some thirty carvings exquisitely done in high-relief on jaguar or deer bones, many of which had backgrounds encrusted with turquoise. The art of fine mosaic was a great Mixtec speciality, and although several pieces featuring this work had disintegrated, the turquoise-covered skull is still intact. Knives of obsidian or volcanic glass, and jewellery made from jade, shells, jet and amber were also found.

Yet of all the different substances worked by the Mixtec, it was with gold and silver that they excelled. Excavated from the tomb were armlets and ear-rings, bells and necklaces in which each bead represented a turtle or the teeth of the jaguar. There was also the golden crown with its plume of gold which Caso

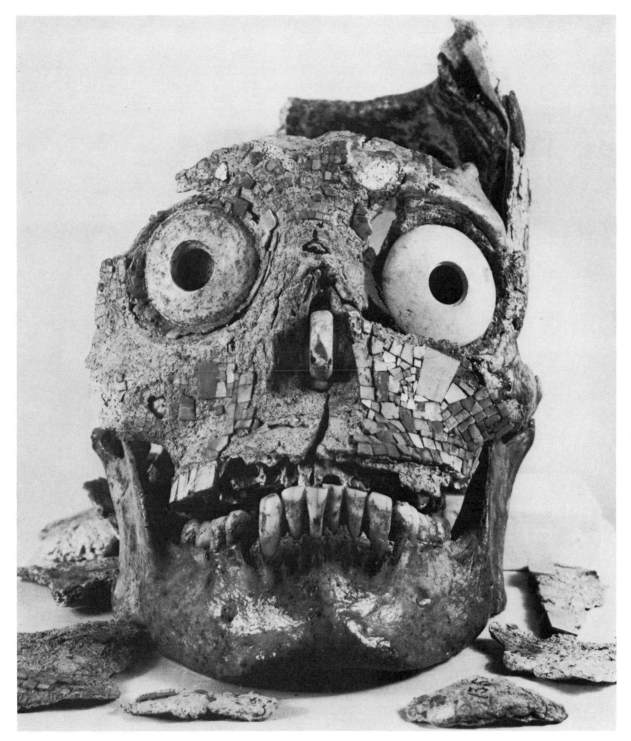

Mixtec skull covered with turquoise mosaic from Tomb 7, Monte Albán

Above Three of the many carved jaguar bones found in Tomb 7 at Monte Albán

Right Mixtec gold pendant representing Mictlantecuhtli, Lord of the Dead, from Tomb 7 at Monte Albán (height $4\frac{1}{2}$ inches) (*see also colour plates 18 and 19*)

Far right Illustrations from Sahagún's manuscript showing some of the pre-bath. Conquest gold-working techniques: casting by the 'lost wax' method, repoussé work, and washing the finished pieces in an alum

mentioned. One of the most extraordinary pieces discovered was a great breast-plate in the form of a 'jaguar-knight' which showed a human head wearing a jaguar-like helmet with imitation feathers of gold thread. Suspended from the neck is a collar with a small bird.

No less spectacular is a gold pendant $4\frac{1}{2}$ in high, made in the image of Mictlantecuhtili, the Lord of the Dead. The base consists of two plaques inscribed with glyphs, and these have enabled Caso to place the offerings and the burial somewhere in the fifteenth century. The patron of goldsmiths was Xipe Totec, the Zapotec God of Spring, and it is only fitting that he too should have been portrayed. A small mask, only $3\frac{1}{4}$ in in height, vividly shows the skin of the victim worn by this deity, otherwise known as 'The Flayed One'. During ritual ceremonies to make the earth fruitful, the priest representing Xipe Totec would don the human skin that represented the earth's springtime covering of green, and which the Mixtec further identified with the sheets of gold often used by jewellers.

This goldware marked the zenith of the art of metal-working in ancient Mexico. The Mixtec elaborated a number of different processes, and a highly detailed account of these various techniques is contained in the manuscript entitled '*La Historia General de las Cosas de la Nueva España*' or 'The General History of the Things of New Spain', which was compiled over a period of eleven years following the Conquest by the Spanish friar, Bernardino de Sahagún. The metal-working procedures which he described include smelting, welding, inlaying or incising, filigree and repoussé, in which elaborate designs were embossed onto thin sheets of gold or silver. All this was accomplished with a minimum of wood, copper or stone tools. Another technique which the Mixtec mastered to perfection was that of casting by the lost wax method. A core of clay was covered with beeswax, modelled and carved into the desired shape. This was then covered with a layer of clay and heated. When the wax had melted it was poured out, and molten metal was substituted and left to harden.

Most of these techniques have long been forgotten by the Indians of Oaxaca. The prohibitions of the *Conquistadores* saw to that. But the old idols are once again being made, replicas of ancient masterpieces, for the ever-expanding tourist trade. Juan Lopez Armengol and his brother Andrés live in a small village just five kilometres outside the City of Oaxaca, and together they carry on the family business. Much of Juan's work consists of making replicas for a wholesaler who keeps him regularly supplied with the gold he needs and who later sells his work. A skilled craftsman by contemporary standards, (though not perhaps by the standard of the Mixtec of old). Juan solders individual sections together with a blowlamp, filing down any rough edges and dipping the finished replica in a chemical bath to bring a shine to the gold.

The silver jewellery which Andrés makes is, however, in a more recent Indian tradition. With a fretsaw he cuts out prancing horses, turkeys, lizards and scorpions from the sheets of silver that he buys from a bank in Oaxaca City. These shapes are then placed on a board covered with beeswax which holds them firm while he embosses them, or incises them with decorative patterning. Later these tiny silver creatures are combined with red porcelain beads and made into necklaces or long dangling ear-rings of the kind popular with Indian women throughout the region.

The ingenuity and vitality of the Mexican artisan found a new source of inspiration in tin, a metal introduced after the Conquest, and in Oaxaca City a number of families earn a living by working with this inexpensive and readily-available metal. José Velasco, his wife Juana and their son Aarón take it in turns to cut out the sheet metal with sharp shears, and to hammer out the various segments on a block, incising or embossing them. Later these are soldered together and the finished pieces painted by Juana, using bright and translucent colours. Purple suns, smiling moons, ornate mirror frames, red and yellow churches, Noah's arks, miniature rocking horses, ornamental fruit trees and enormous vases of flowers fill the rambling workshop and overgrown patio of the Velasco family.

But although the Spaniards brought with them a whole range of technical innovations and new materials, they also initiated an era of destruction. Spanish soldiers, merchants and missionaries took control of Mexico, dispossessing the Indian rulers and priests, and by 1564 the first Archbiship of Mexico was able to congratulate himself on the smashing of 20,000 idols and the demolition of 500 temples. On these ruins, churches and cathedrals were erected. In Oaxaca, where the conquest proved rapid and easy, numbers of codices were destroyed as works of superstition and black magic, and at Mitla several ancient buildings were broken up during the building of

the Colonial Church that stands to this day, surrounded by the remains of a Mixtec temple.

Today the Mixtec number over 300,000. They refer to themselves in their own language as 'The People of the Rain': the name by which outsiders know them was taken by the Spanish from the Aztec language. When they saw the mountainous and misty territory inhabited by the Mixtec, the Aztec called it 'Mixtecapan' or 'Place of the Clouds', and the Spanish Conquistadores abbreviated the word to 'La Mixteca'. This area which covers over 14,000 sq miles and ranges from the high mountains of Oaxaca and estern Guerrero to the Pacific coastal plain, comprises three distinct geographical zones.

It is the Mixteca Alta or Mountain region that has the highest number of Mixtec inhabitants, with an average of thirty to every square mile. This rugged area, whose long rainy season lasts from April right through to October, encompasses abrupt slopes, narrow but fertile valleys, jagged peaks, a few unnavigable rivers, prairies and even a cold and dry desert. Sudden changes in the altitude make for strong variations in climate over short distances. Although tracks and footpaths cross the region, there are still relatively few roads, and it remains one of the most isolated in Mexico.

The Mixtec, who live here alongside other Indian groups,

farm the land much as their ancestors did. Fields are cleared by cutting down trees or shrubs and burning them. Seeds are planted from mid-March to April, immediately after the rains have begun, with the aid of a digging stick. The oxen and plough introduced by Spanish settlers are only of use in lowland areas, where it is not unusual for poorer Indians to rent a team of oxen from neighbours richer than themselves. Maize, beans and squash are the staple crops. Often planted in the same field, they are harvested between August and December, depending on the altitude. In some climates maize is cultivated twice yearly. When the earth becomes impoverished, land is left fallow for four to five years. This pattern of subsistence agriculture demands considerable mobility of the farmer, who may often have to walk one or even two hours to reach his fields, and in some areas it is common practice for the entire family to move to a temporary home during the planting season.

Today as in the past, maize is the staple food of the Mixtec people. Made into *tortillas*, it accompanies the beans, the chili peppers that highlanders buy from lowlanders, the tomatoes, the onions and the green vegetables that form the average daily diet. Meat is a luxury. Although families often keep turkeys and chickens, or more rarely sheep and goats, these are generally eaten on ceremonial occasions only. Over recent years game has become increasingly scarce: in coastal areas a few deer may still be found, but the mountain hunter is restricted to catching rabbits with traps and to killing small birds such as partridges with the *cerbatana* or pre-Conquest blowpipe. Fishing is unusual in the highlands, but lizards, snakes and even grasshoppers are eaten occasionally.

Life is hard in the Mixteca, and laziness is shunned. Women rise early, often before dawn, to prepare *tortillas* for the men who set off for the fields as soon as they have eaten. Although there are government schools in some communities, in remoter areas it is still usual for sons to accompany their fathers, and it is expected that by the time they reach adolescence they will be able to work the land alone if necessary. Daughters stay at home with their mothers, learning to do domestic tasks through play when small. But by the age of seven they will already be helping to grind maize, herding sheep if the family own any, feeding the poultry, bringing water from the nearby well or river, and minding baby brothers and sisters.

Mixtec houses from the coastal area of Oaxaca

Although in low-lying areas the Mixtec sometimes live in close-knit communities or small towns, in the mountains houses tend to be scattered among fields, cut off from one another by quite long distances. Often built high on slopes, highland homes are rectangular with sloping roofs of palm thatch or tiles, and walls of *abode* or wattle and daub. In low-lying areas they are similar, but often round. Measuring about twelve by fifteen feet, the average Mixtec house consists of a single room with one entrance and no windows. The floor is of earth, and furnishings are sparse. They include a few low chairs, pegs in the wall for belongings, and palm mats which the family use to sleep on at night but keep rolled up in a corner during the day. Additional possessions may be stowed away among the beams, and food is stored in hanging baskets. Usually cooking is done outside, but if the house includes a kitchen area, then an outlet for smoke is left between the walls and the roof.

Many communities are entirely self-sufficient, but a number of villages have tended to specialise in a particular craft, improving their meagre economy by selling their wares. In the highlands, palm weaving is a widespread craft. Men intertwine the long strands while walking to their fields, and the women

Weaving on a waist-strap loom in the
Mixtec village of San Juan Colorado

do likewise as they go on errands or sit at home, resting in between their domestic duties. Sons and daughters are expected to learn by imitation. Whether grown locally or brought for its finer quality from other Indians in the next state, the palm is stored underground to keep it moist before being woven into baskets, mats, rain capes and hats. Often the production of hats amounts to a regular cottage industry, with *mestizo* contractors buying up large quantities to resell in tourist centres such as Acapulco.

Pottery is another important craft. Strictly utilitarian and contrasting sadly with the magnificent polychrome ware produced before the Conquest, contemporary Mixtec pottery is made principally by women. Techniques are more primitive than is the case with the Zapotec Indians: no moulds or wheels are used to model the local clay into jars for storing food and water, cooking pots, vessels for eating or griddles for heating *tortillas*. Simple in form and largely undecorated, the pots are sun-dried and later fired in great open-air bonfires.

One craft that has remained virtually unchanged, losing none of its vitality and intricacy, is that of weaving on a waist-strap loom. This technique is still used extensively throughout the region. The loom looks little more than a bundle of sticks when dismantled. While one end is attached to a tree or post, the other fits around the waist of the weaver, who works from a sitting or kneeling position. Weaving is a woman's task, done whenever time permits, and in remote areas the entire family is clothed with garments from her loom. Cotton, cultivated by the Mixtec of the Coast, is bought by mountain people who also use the wool from their sheep. Both are spun with a spindle in a half gourd or clay dish. Local dyes such as the indigo plant are still popular, but rarer dyes are sometimes obtained through trade. Cochineal, which was in great demand before the Conquest and later sold internationally by the Spaniards, is derived from a tiny parasite which yields a brilliant crimson when crushed.

Handwoven textiles are long-wearing and ideally suited to the Mixtec climate and way of life. They are also beautiful. Decorative motifs range from stylised representations of animals to geometric bands in bright colours, which are incorporated into the cloth during weaving. Designs often have a magical function, protecting the wearer from harm. Pregnant women who live by the Coast trust in the woven patterning of their waist-sashes to ward off the Rainbow of the East who is

Mixtec weaver from Jamiltepec selling her textiles at the market

believed to harm unborn children.

Weavers work without a pattern. Instead they draw on their memory and their own innate sense of design, formed by centuries of tradition. Female dress still includes the pre-Conquest '*huipil*' which is a tunic-like garment allowing great freedom of movement. It is often left unsewn at the sides, so that mothers can more easily suckle their babies. Throughout the Mixteca, the *huipil* generally hangs loosely over a wrap-around skirt which is held in place by a long waist-sash. Men, like women, own two or three changes of clothing. But unlike women, they tend to travel more widely outside the region and so their dress has become more European in style. The sashes that hold up their loose-fitting trousers are often highly decorated however, and are reminiscent of the elaborate loincloths of the past.

In the Mixteca, as in all other regions of Mexico where indigenous clothing has been retained, each village has its own particular variation, and this enables Indians instantly to identify each other's group and place of origin. In each community a weaver's work can instantly be recognised as her own, despite the fact that design elements rarely deviate from the village tradition. Mothers teach their daughters to

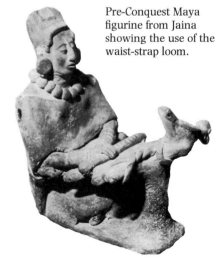

Pre-Conquest Maya figurine from Jaina showing the use of the waist-strap loom.

The People of the Valley 115

weave early in life, for it is a much valued accomplishment, and women who do not possess it are obliged to purchase or barter for their costumes. In many areas weavers regard their *huipiles* as wealth, considering the months taken to weave one as an investment of time and skill. The more ornate the costume, the more prestige it brings the wearer, and during fiestas women often wear two or even three *huipiles* at once. The weaver's pride in her work reaches even beyond the grave, for when she dies she will be buried in her finest and most treasured *huipil*.

The Mixtec view death much as their ancestors did, thinking of it as a long journey. Corpses are placed in wooden coffins, or quite simply wrapped in palm mats and buried. As well as being dressed in their best clothing, the dead are given their favourite tools and a supply of food, both for themselves and for any animals they may encounter. Sometimes small sums of money are also included. Burials are accompanied by music, dancing and feasting.

Notions about the afterlife are vague, but the Mixtec are clear about their own position in the universe. Life is difficult and they must work hard. Survival depends on the forces of nature, and these can either help man or harm him if sufficient respect is not shown. In the Mixteca land is regarded as a living and personalised force, and offerings are often made to the crops. There are also rain dances and pre-planting rain rituals in caves accompanied by music, the burning of copal resin and even animal sacrifice. It is this devotion to their land that unifies the Mixtec as a race. Pre-Conquest figurines, made by their ancestors, are still unearthed in their fields, and the Mixtec guard them reverently, believing them to be the gods of the people who inhabited the land before them.

Another all-important link which the Mixtec possess with their past is their language. In remote mountain areas there are still villages where up to eighty per cent of the population speak no Spanish at all. This is how one young Mixtec woman, living in the highlands, sums up the situation:

> I don't have another language to speak. I just don't know any other. Here I am with my children, and they too speak Mixtec. When my baby grows up, I shall send him to the school in the next village. Perhaps there he'll learn how to speak Spanish, because I can't teach him. My eldest son already goes, but he just plays and learns nothing. As for my daughter, she's afraid to go because of the horses and sheep she has to pass on the way.

Mixtec women at the market in Pinotepa Nacional

Asked how she and her family live, she replies: 'I keep my family fed. When I have time I weave, and sometimes I sell my work. Then I can buy food for my family: chili peppers and beans. We have no sheep, you see, and very little money. Life is hard for us.'

But difficult though life may often be for both the Mixtec and the Zapotec who today inhabit Oaxaca, religious faith still plays a dominant role in their lives. Celestino Cruz, the woodcarver from San Martín Tilcajete, holds very definite views about this:

> We all think that we are not idolaters as our forefathers were. They worshipped the God of Maize, the God of the Sun, the God of Stone, the God of the Trees, the God of the Mountains. There were many things that they adored as their gods. But today I think it is just the same. Because today we carry on adoring the Virgin of Solitude, the Virgin of Jaquila, the Virgin of Guadalupe, Our Lord of Esquipulas and so on. And that is why I think we are and will continue to be idolators.

This strange mixture of past and present can best be seen in the Zapotec Feather Dance. Performed today in honour of San Martín, the Patron Saint of Celestino's village, it enacts the Spanish Conquest of Mexico. But its roots stretch back in time, and scholars have suggested that an earlier version of this dance may have belonged to the cult of Macuilxochtli, the

The ancient Zapotec Feather Dance being performed in the village of San Martín Tilcajete (*see also colour plate 34*)

ancient god of music, dance and song. Dancers who take the roles of Montezuma and his warriors wear elaborate and colourful costumes with enormous plumed head-dresses reminiscent of crested birds.

The inhabitants of San Martín Tilcajete know little of the history of the Feather Dance, but they perform it regularly in the square outside the church. Celestino explains why:

> This dance is very important to us, because it is a tradition we have always kept during our festivals and fiestas. There was a time when our forefathers stopped performing, but then the dance was organised once again, and I hope we will never again stop performing it at our fiestas.

During his exile in Mexico City, Celestino looks forward to the fiesta when he will return to his village, put on his costume and take his part in the dance. 'I've always felt very strongly about the dance ever since I was a small boy of perhaps ten. I can remember my mother explaining to me that my father had a part in the dance, and I longed to have one too. My father played the role of Montezuma, and I still hope that one day I shall do the same.'

Dancers pay the musicians' fees and provide their own costumes. The expense can be considerable, but there is not a single dancer who would lose the honour of performing. In addition there is the religious commitment. As Celestino explains: 'We dance because we have taken a vow to do so. We have promised the Saints. And when we dance, we are dancing on behalf of all the villagers—they are demanding that we dance.'

For the ancient races that once peopled Mexico, to dance was to pray. And as Celestino and his companions perform the complicated steps of the dance, moving to the strident sounds of the local brass band and shaking their gourd rattles, they are reliving Mexico's past. The villagers look on as Cortés and Montezuma confront one another, each surrounded by his followers. The dancing is interspersed with passages of dialogue, well rehearsed over the years.

Above Celestino Cruz wearing the headdress of brightly dyed chicken feathers; *below* Performers taking the part of the *Conquistadores*, who now feature prominently in the dance

> Now I am going to make my narration
> To all those who are gathered here,
> And I ask you to forgive me
> For my rustic voice and language.
> According to our ancient history
> This is the sad and pitiful story
> Of the imprisonment of King Montezuma.

The wooden swords of the combatants are brandished, and as the battle rages, Montezuma declaims:

> Oh the cowardly lie of your damned betrayal,
> It breaks my heart to lose my land!

And Cortés replies:

> Throughout America the rays of the Spanish sun
> Are going to spread.
> With the sound of battle the idol-worshippers
> Will be brought down.

Finally, after many hours of fierce fighting, the Mexican warriors are vanquished. Montezuma takes the cross and loses his lands and all his treasures.

The People of the Valley 119

4 The People of the Rainforest

While the inhabitants of Monte Albán were forging their distinctive civilisation in Oaxaca, and while the ceremonial centres of Teotihuacán in Central Mexico and El Tajín on the Gulf Coast were expanding, another civilisation was flourishing to the south and south-east—that of the Maya. These unique and highly gifted peoples gave rise over the centuries to one of the most brilliant cultures of the New World, surpassing all other Middle American peoples in their knowledge of mathematics and astronomy, and in the complexity of their calendar systems. That they were also great builders and sculptors is shown by the many temples, palaces and plazas which have survived together with exquisite carvings of stone and jade.

At its height this astonishing civilisation covered over 117,000 sq miles, an area as immense as it was varied. Pine-clad mountain ranges with misty peaks that rise to a height of nearly 13,000 ft, fertile valleys, tropical rainforests and dry limestone plains were all included within the Maya territories. These stretched across what are now the Mexican states of Tabasco. Chiapas, Campeche and Quintana Roo, taking in the Yucatán Peninsula and reaching out across Belize and Guatemala into the Western parts of Honduras and El Salvador. By AD 200 stone monuments had already begun to appear in Southern Mexico, a sign that the civilisation of the Maya was well underway, and their achievements were to span the intervening centuries leading up to the Conquest. But despite intensive study, the origins of the Maya remain a mystery. The history of man in the Maya area extends back into the early hunting period. The oldest artefact so far found there is a small projectile point of obsidian, unearthed not by archaeologists but by a schoolboy on a picnic in the hills just west of Guatemala City. This stone point confirms that the highlands were occupied between 12,000 and 10,000 years ago by nomadic bands of hunters and gatherers.

The Popol Vuh, the great epic of the Quiché Maya of

The Lake of Najá, deep in the rainforests of Chiapas

Guatemala, which was fortunately recorded in Colonial times, gives a poetic explanation of their beginnings:

This is an account of how everything was in suspense, at peace, in silence, immobile, quiet, and the expanse of the heavens was empty.

This is the first account, the first discourse. There was not yet a man, neither were there animals, birds, fish, crabs, trees, stones, caves, ravines, greenery or woodland; there was only sky.

Before the face of the earth appeared, there was only motionless sea, and a great emptiness of sky. . . .

There was only stillness and silence in the darkness, in the night. Only the Creator, the Maker, Tepeu, Gucumatz, the Forefathers, were in the water surrounded by clarity. . . .

'Let the emptiness fill, they said. Let the water weave its way downward so the earth can show its face. Let there be light. Let the dawn rise over heavens and earth. There can be no glory, no splendour, until the human creature exists, and man is formed.' Thus they spoke.

And then they made the earth. That, in truth, was how the earth was created. 'Earth', they cried. And in an instant it was there.

Like the mist, like the clouds, like a puff of dust was the creation. . . .

This ancient myth goes on to describe man's origins. Having endowed the earth with animals and plants, the forefather gods felt the need to be praised and venerated, so they made man-like creatures from mud, but to mud they returned. Next the creators called into being a race of wooden figures, and these multiplied. They proved stupid and ungrateful, however, so the gods sent a black rain of pitch to punish and destroy them. The pots, grinding-stones and animals that had belonged to the wooden manikins took part in their destruction. 'You treated us ill,' they said, 'and now we will do the same to you.' Only a few of the wooden men escaped, and they became monkeys. Finally true men, the ancestors of the Quiché Indians, were created from maize dough.

Not surprisingly, historians have been anxious to piece together a more factual version of the beginnings of Maya civilisation, and there are a number of conflicting theories on the subject. Linguistic evidence suggests that the very first Maya may have been a small tribe of North American origin, but if so their long migration across Mexico is surrounded by conjecture. One theory maintains that the tribe stopped during its wanderings in southern Veracruz and northern Tabasco, sharing in the early Olmec culture when it emerged around the tenth century BC. The ancestors of the Maya would then have continued their journey towards the east and south, taking with them a number of Olmec cultural traits, and leaving behind a group of Indians known as the Huastec who now inhabit a large part of Veracruz and Tamaulipas, cut off from the rest of the Maya family although speaking a language which is linked with theirs.

An alternative and perhaps more widely accepted theory suggests that this early tribe migrated from North America, moving southwards until it reached the highlands of Guatemala by the middle of the third millennium BC. Over the next thousand years two groups would have split away, with the Yucatec moving into the lowland plains of the peninsula, and the Huastec settling in the Gulf Coast area which they occupy today, totally separated from their linguistic kinsmen. Gradually other groups would have followed suit, leaving the Guatemalan highlands in favour of Chiapas and other regions. With time, the languages spoken by these different Maya tribes would have evolved, becoming in many cases mutually unintelligible. So far archaeologists have been unable to provide conclusive evidence to support either theory. Unfavourable geological conditions and the often dense vegetation have severely hampered their search for early remains.

In the Mexican state of Chiapas, artefacts discovered at the rock shelter of Santa Marta have provided information about later settlers. Querns and grinding stones, thought to be between nine and five thousand years old, tell us that seeds and other plants had become a regular source of food, although the accompanying projectile points show that their users were still keen hunters. It seems likely that domesticated strains of maize began to spread southwards from Central Mexico from 5000 BC onwards, and an analysis of pollen, recovered after four thousand years from the bottom of a lake in the Petén region of Guatemala, has proved that this cereal was being cultivated in the area by 2000 BC. There is good archaeological evidence that about this time these early hunters and gatherers were grouping themselves into small and scattered villages, concentrating upon agriculture for their support; this marks the first really intensive settlement of the area. Recent work carried out by Dr Norman Hammond in Belize suggests that some of these early settlements were already recognisably Maya.

This new sedentary way of life allowed skills such as potting to develop, although not all village cultures progressed at the same rhythm. Ocós in Guatemala was a particularly early site. Here, on the hot and fertile coast of the Pacific, jars and flat-bottomed bowls have been excavated, their clay surfaces often stamped with decorative patterning. Female figurines of clay, thought to have been associated with the fertility of the crops, suggest that ceremonialism was evolving, and a mound found nearby is believed to have served as a temple platform. Another series of artefacts, dating from the fifth or fourth century BC and unearthed at Las Charcas in the Valley of Guatemala, shows how craft skills had improved by this time. Finds include remnants of woven textiles, basketry, matting, fragments of rope and examples of a very refined type of pottery decorated with red-painted designs. But although these advances were to form a base upon which Maya culture could evolve, there is nothing to suggest that these early settlers had even a rudimentary notion of sculpture, architecture, mathematics, hieroglyphic writing or the other arts over which their successors were to achieve such mastery.

While these simple farming communities were slowly developing in the south, however, the great civilisation of the Olmec had already begun to expand on the Gulf Coast. In this hot and humid area, their extraordinary ceremonial centres were appearing, first at San Lorenzo and later at La Venta. Gradually the different cultural traits of this mighty and mysterious civilisation began to spread, filtering through to lesser peasant cultures in other parts of Mexico. Did the Olmec influence spread to the early Maya in a similar way? Or had it already been carried south, as some historians claim, by migrating groups who shared in the Olmec culture before continuing their journey and settling the Maya lands? Alternatively, as the recent evidence from Belize suggests, did Maya civilisation evolve independently in pre-Olmec times? It is not yet possible to answer these questions, but an Olmec influence is clearly visible in Chiapas and Guatemala at a number of sites, where a newly-emerged but already elaborate art style both recalls Olmec monuments while foreshadowing future achievements among the Classic Maya.

Izapa, on the Pacific coastal plain of Chiapas, belongs to this formative period and has given its name to the style of art found there. It is a huge ceremonial complex with over eighty earthen mounds and a number of stone monuments carved in high relief to show gods and busy scenes from daily life. Although these carvings are more cluttered than those of the Olmec, there are many links with this great culture including the portrayal of the were-jaguar. This deity harks back to the Olmec jaguar-god with its possible associations with rain and lightning, but may also be a forerunner of Chac, the raingod of the later Maya. Still on the Pacific coastal plain but further south at El Baúl another monument in the style of Izapa has been found. It is an upright stone slab, or stela, which bears witness to the growing preoccupation of these ancient peoples with time. Thought by many to be one of the earliest dated monuments within the

Carved stone monument from Izapa

Maya area, its carved surface shows a figure in profile. Wearing a plumed head-dress and holding a spear, he stands facing two vertical columns of glyphs. Although many of the signs remain undecipherable, archaeologists have calculated that the calendrical glyphs give a date which corresponds to AD 36 in our calendar.

Other sites in Guatemala have provided additional information about life at this early period. Kaminaljuyú, in the highlands, had over 200 earth mounds which presupposes an ordered society where rulers could call on a disciplined labour force. The excavation of a particularly lavish tomb, constructed as a rectangular, stepped shaft let into the summit of one of these mounds, confirms that rulers were treated with great respect. The corpse, covered with cinnabar pigment, was buried with a profusion of offerings that included pottery and marble vessels, soapstone bottles and jade carvings. The tomb was then covered with a wooden floor and later superimposed temple platforms were built over it. This early use of pyramids as funerary monuments was to set a precedent for later Maya cultures. In addition to their architectural achievements, the élite at Kaminaljuyú were both numerate and literate. Monuments, in the style of Izapa, are decorated with carved glyphs that have yet to be deciphered.

Drawing of the stela from El Baúl

The peoples of the highlands and the Pacific Coast were steadily progressing, but in the great forests of the lowlands advances were being made which would ultimately prove still more important. In the Petén area of Guatemala, ambitious ceremonial centres with large temple mounds began to appear in cleared areas of the rainforest. At Uaxactún a massive platform has been found, dating from this formative period. Faced with white stucco, it was inset on each of its four sides with imposing stairways, and supported a temple of wooden poles and thatch. Even more elaborate structures have been excavated at Tikal, many with the remains of painted stucco on their outer walls. Archaeologists have also discovered a burial chamber, with offerings as splendid and as varied as those found at the highland site of Kaminaljuyú. Even this early on in their development, however, the lowland Maya were taking a rather different course from that of the highlanders. Their unique style of building was determined not only by their forest environment, but also by the vast deposits of limestone characteristic of the region. Assured of an inexhaustible supply

General view of Tikal in Guatemala (*c.* AD 200–700)

of easily cut building materials, these early architects were able to create unexpectedly elaborate constructions which were faced with stucco made from burned and ground limestone, mixed with water. Yet despite their achievements as builders, there is little evidence to suggest at this early period that the lowland Maya made as much use of a hieroglyphic system as highlanders, or that they were as concerned with recording dates.

It is difficult to assess from these outward signs what turns social organisation and religion were taking, but it seems safe to assume that in all these different ceremonial centres a pantheon of gods was being worshipped, possibly derived, like the Izapa art-style, from the Olmec, and similar to the pantheon venerated throughout most of central and southern Mexico at this time. With the emergence of a priesthood, worship would have become formalised, finding expression in art and architecture, and in the highlands promoting the development of writing, mathematics and calendar systems. As Maya beliefs crystallised, small local communities were welded together into larger more stable ones, with priest-aristocrats ruling over the peasant farmers. Unlike some of the great urban centres of northern Mexico, these ceremonial centres were occupied only by the élite, while the farming population, which provided the food and the labour for their construction and upkeep, lived outside. But in the same way that Cuicuilco or Teotihuacán heralded the start of a new age in the north, to the south the advances made at Tikal, Uaxactún or Kaminaljuyú were destined to pave the way for the great city states of the Maya. From these mysterious but promising beginnings their civilisation was to evolve, embarking in the third century AD on a period of artistic and intellectual expansion that was to last for the next six hundred years.

For the Maya time was an all-consuming preoccupation. The highlanders had already shown their concern with recording dates, but among the lowlanders this awareness of time was later to become of overwhelming importance. Past and future receded in endless vistas of hundreds and thousands of years, as the ancient Maya tried to measure the passage of time and to solve its mysteries. Most major cultures in Middle America used both a solar and a ritual calendar. But although the Maya shared a number of basic principles with these other cultures, they were to surpass them all with their advanced knowledge of astronomy and mathematics. By observing the length of the lunar cycles, the equinoxes and solstices, the revolutions of the planet Venus and the passage of the seasons, the Maya were able to evolve their own highly elaborate and precise systems for recording time.

The solar calendar of 365 days was organised into eighteen months of twenty days each, with an additional period of five days which were held to be unlucky. Their religious calendar, known as the *tzolkin*, was composed of twenty day-names which were combined with thirteen numbers to make a cycle of 260 days. The permutation of these two calendars gave the 'Calendar Round' of fifty-two years, this being the minimum time in which any one date could be repeated. The Maya also devised two other time cycles, both the result of extremely long-term astronomical observation. One of these was a Venus calendar, while the other was lunar. As if not entirely satisfied with these systems, the Maya went on to develop the 'Long Count' which enabled them to work with much longer time spans. Although this dating procedure may initially have been invented by the Olmec, the Maya were to carry it to unparalleled heights of refinement. It worked as a day-to-day calendar, which ran from some fixed point in the far distant past. The correlation between Maya and Christian dating systems is an extremely complex problem, but some scholars have suggested that this fixed point may have been the year 3113 BC. Quite what the Maya would have wanted to record with this date, other than perhaps the Creation, it is hard to imagine. With the help of these different systems, the Maya were able to calculate periods of up to 90,000,000 years, and modern investigators have concluded that the margin of error was just one day in every 6000 years.

This obsession with time of the Maya priest-astronomers was not an end in itself. Rather, it was a way of foreseeing the future, and sprang from a deep spiritual anxiety. Every day in the *Tzolkin* or ritual calendar had its own omens and associations, with the fate of mankind depending on a successful balance of divine influences. The Maya believed that cycles repeated themselves, and by recording dates they felt able to understand the forces of destiny and to prepare for the future.

Dates were recorded on free-standing stone monuments, or stelae. These were often carved in high relief, and began to appear in profusion from around AD 300 at all the leading

Stela from Copán in Honduras. Glyphs surround two standing figures

19 Gold mask representing the god Xipe Totec. Mixtec. Height 3¼ inches (*p. 109*).

18 Gold pectoral representing the god Xiuhtecuhtli. Mixtec (*p. 109*).

'We shouldn't undervalue what our ancestors left for us'

20 *Above*: Olmec figurines forming a ceremonial group. Approx. 8 inches high. La Venta *c* 900 BC (*p. 33*).

21 *Right*: Maya carving on a lintel from Yaxchilán. *c* AD 720 (*p. 132*).

22 Terracotta figures with characteristic 'baby-face' Olmec features (*p. 33*).

23 *Below left and right*: Details from wall paintings dating from *c* AD 750, recently discovered at Cacaxla (*p. 21*).

24 to 28 Jaguar or 'Tiger' Dance, performed in honour of the patron saint of Totoltepec village, Guerrero (*p. 34*).

'At least let us have flowers . . .

29 & 30 Dance of the *Voladores* or 'Flyers', performed by the Totonac at El Tajín (*p. 49*).

31 The Night of the Dead, celebrated throughout Mexico on 2 November (*p. 53*).

. . . at least let us have singing'

32 & 33 Nahua festivities in Cuetzalan, Puebla. *Above*: Traditional hair style with purple wool. *Right*: Quetzal Dance (*p. 81*).

34 The Feather Dance performed in the Zapotec village of San Martín Tilcajete, Oaxaca, re-enacting the Spanish Conquest of Mexico (*p. 117*).

35 & 36 The Mayo Indians of Sonora performing Easter ceremonies. *Left*: Pharisee in goat-skin mask. *Above*: Followers of Pontius Pilate (*pp. 177–9*).

37 Huichol women taking part in the annual *peyote* festival in the mountains of Jalisco (*p. 216*).

38 Huichol *'nierika'* or yarn painting, inspired by the visions that the gods send during *peyote* rituals. In this picture Father Sun presides over a ceremony conducted in his honour by the shaman and his assistant in front of the temple (*p. 217*).

ceremonial centres of the lowlands. Elaborate scenes, sometimes featuring gods and rulers, were combined with calendrical inscriptions. These were headed by an introductory glyph, representing the profile or symbol of one of the nine gods who governed dates, followed by glyphs representing the required date. The Maya also made use of the common Middle-American system of showing numbers by means of dots and bars, with one as their basic unit. The concept of zero, which constituted a major breakthrough in the Middle American field of mathematics, was portrayed by a stylised shell. Using these glyphs and symbols, the ancient Maya recorded on their stelae in Long Count the number of elapsed cycles since the start of their chronology, often adding the solar and lunar cycles for extra precision.

The *Popol Vuh*, with its tale of the Creation, was not the only Maya epic to survive the Spanish Conquest. A second, the *Chilam Balam*, talks of history, astronomy and the calendar. This passage, from the Chumayel version, gives an insight into the importance which time had for the ancient Maya—a people who had integrated their existence with the cosmos.

Detail from a Maya stela showing a counting system in which a dot corresponds to one, and a bar to five

> Complete was the month; complete, the year; complete, the day; complete, the breath of life as it passed also; complete, the blood, when they [our ancestors] arrived at their beds, their mats, their thrones. In due measure did they recite the good prayers; in due measure they sought the lucky days, until they saw the good stars enter into their reign; then they kept watch while the reign of the good stars began. Then everything was good.

Throughout this period of Maya florescence, the arts of construction and sculpture were closely linked with the sciences of mathematics and astronomy. In the Petén area of Guatemala, where vast swamps, lakes and grassland alternate with tall tropical rainforests, the great lowland centres of Uaxactún and Tikal continued to grow outwards and upwards. At Tikal, now partly restored, six great temple pyramids flanked with steep stairways rose to heights of over 200 ft above the level of the plazas they enclosed. Further south in what is now Honduras, a magnificent complex of pyramids, temples, terraces and courts appeared at Copán. Even in its ruin, and only partially rescued from the forest, it is a breathtaking sight. The ball court, with markers in the shape of macaw heads, is

Pottery figure of a warrior from the Island
of Jaina (height 7 inches)

widely thought to be the most perfect known for this era among the Maya, and the stone carvings in the round that decorate the site distinguish it from all others.

The great forests that nurtured these imposing city-states in Guatemala and Honduras also reach far into Mexico. At Yaxchilán, beside the brown and fast-flowing waters of the Usumacinta river, another impressive lowland centre grew up. The site has changed very little since it was rediscovered

Maya stela from Copán in Honduras

towards the middle of the last century by intrepid travellers, fired by rumours of a lost city hidden by the jungle. Today there is a bumpy grass airstrip in a nearby clearing, and a scattering of homes for the custodians who ward off looters. But apart from these few concessions to the twentieth century, it has been left virtually untouched. Built around AD 550, the centre of Yaxchilán stands as it has stood for centuries, ruined and deserted. Tall ceibas, mahoganies, zapotes, palms and cedars surround the palaces and the temples, sending out great roots as if waiting for the opportunity to close in once again. In the clearings, where sunlight filters through the trees, carved monuments lie overgrown with moss and grasses.

The builders of Yaxchilán were concerned less with height than with decoration, and the temples that top the stair-flanked pyramids are beautifully ornamented with roof combs, while figures in stucco and stone adorn the upper façades. Here the Maya of the forest would congregate for festivals, markets and religious rites. Our chief source of information about these people and their rulers is a series of stone lintels, exquisitely carved in high relief. Among their scenes of conquest and ceremonial life are dates, and other glyphic texts, because in addition to their chronological and mathematical symbols, the ancient Maya evolved a form of literary writing which they often used to accompany their calendric notations. This hieroglyphic system was the most advanced and complex in Middle America, and it has proved extremely difficult to decipher. Many attempts have been made, some even involving the use of a computer, and it is no longer true, as it was only thirty years ago, to say that Maya writing cannot be read. However, at present only a number of phrases and name-glyphs have been identified.

Maya hieroglyphs were both ideographic and phonetic. Unlike pictograms, which show only the thing referred to, ideograms can express abstract concepts not easy to visualise. In addition, the Maya gave their symbols a phonetic significance, so that ideograms could sometimes be used for their sound-value. In this way, a sign could have several associations. The subject matter of these hieroglyphic texts is still a matter for debate. The late Sir Eric Thompson, the British Mayanist, believed that they dealt exclusively with time, astronomy, gods and ceremonies. Research carried out by Tatiana Proskouriakoff, however, seems to suggest that some

Detail of a stone lintel from Yaxchilán (*see also colour plate 21*)

texts were also concerned with historic events such as victories and dynastic successions. The Yaxchilán lintels figure very prominently in her investigations, enabling her to reconstruct the history of an extremely militant 'Jaguar' Dynasty which ruled the site in the eighth century, and was followed in AD 725 by the Dynasty of the 'Bird Jaguar'.

All memory of these once great and powerful rulers has long since passed away, but the gods of Yaxchilán are still revered

Above The main temple at Yaxchilán, thought by the Lacandón to be the home of the Lord Hachakyum

Right Lacandón family paddling across the lake at Najá in a dugout mahogany canoe (*see also colour plates 2 and 3*)

today. A group of Maya Indians comes from far off to perform sacred rituals in the ruined temples. They are the Lacandón Indians, last survivors of the ancient Maya still living in a traditional way, and sole inheritors of the old beliefs and religious rites.

The name 'Lacandón' is thought to mean 'setters up of stone idols', from the Maya word 'Acantún'. If so, it was a pejorative term originally applied to them by other Maya groups at the time of the Conquest. In their own language, however, the Lacandón talk of themselves as the 'Hach Winik' which means 'True Men' or 'Original People'. 'True Speech' or 'Real Language' is their term for this language, and it is closely connected with the branch of Maya which is still spoken today

134 *Of Gods and Men*

by the Yucatec Maya of the Peninsula. This linguistic link seems to suggest that the Lacandón once belonged to the main Yucatec group, but split away, settling in the forests of Chiapas. Whether they ever took part in the great cultures of the past, or whether they always remained a marginal group, existing alongside Maya civilisation, remains a mystery.

During the Colonial period, the Lacandón managed to retain their independence. While the other Maya groups were subjugated by the Spaniards after years of hard fighting, the Lacandón retreated ever deeper into the tropical rainforest, from which they repulsed the incursions of outsiders and earned for themselves the reputation of being a fierce and warlike tribe. Within their own communities, the stories of battles with the Spaniards became legends to be passed down by word of mouth from generation to generation. In this way they remembered the deaths of their people, caused by the terrible 'thunderbolts' of the foreigners. But neither the thundering of the soldiers' guns nor the preaching of Spanish friars, could break the spirit of the Lacandón, who were eventually left in peace. They were so rarely seen, that outside the forests people began to talk of them as a strange race, and tales circulated of four-breasted women.

Towards the end of the nineteenth century the forest was invaded yet again. This time the outsiders were lumbermen looking for mahogany, and they were joined in this century by '*chicleros*' in search of the rubbery sap, *chicle*, from which chewing gum is made. The Lacandón, who often acted as guides, contracted many of the unfamiliar diseases of the outside world and died in large numbers. For a time the total population dropped as low as two hundred individuals, but it is on the increase again, and it is estimated that around 360 Lacandón now live in the great forests, that cover an area of nearly 10,000 sq. miles.

Although there is a tendency to talk of the Lacandón as a single people, they are in fact split into a southern and a northern group. The two communities live many miles apart, and rarely mix with one another. There are differences in their customs and dress, as well as in their dialect, although for a member of one group to say (as often happens) that he cannot understand the other group is an exaggeration. Over the past few years the divisions that already existed have been further intensified by the late introduction of Christianity among the

Lacandón of the southern group. The death of their elders and the threat of disease left them receptive to the teachings of Protestant missionaries belonging to the Summer School of Linguistics from the USA. Religion has also divided the northern group. The families who live on the shores of Lake Metzabok have even more recently been converted to a form of Seventh Day Adventism. But at Lake Najá, only a few miles away, more than a hundred Lacandón still cling to their old religion. They believe that their gods have served them well in the past, and they see no reason to change.

To this day the Lancandón are not incorporated into the political system of Mexico. At Najá, deep in the heart of the rainforest, they manage their own affairs, relying for guidance on old Chan K'in. He is the 'T'o'ohil', the civil and religious leader, and it is due largely to his wisdom and influence that the people of Najá have retained their sense of community and cultural identity. Chan K'in is over eighty and has passed on the civil leadership to his son, who bears the same name; but he remains responsible for the spiritual welfare of his followers. As the guardian of their ancestral rituals and beliefs, he is concerned that these should not be lost but should be passed on to the younger generation, just as they were to him by his predecessors. Inevitably, over the centuries, many features of ancient Maya civlisation have fallen away, and the esoteric achievements of the priestly élite have been long forgotten. Present-day Lacandón have only a simple understanding of astronomy, while the arts of mathematics, hieroglyphic writing and monumental architecture have dwindled away totally. But despite these losses, some important elements have been saved from the old culture.

Chan K'in, the spiritual leader of the Lacandón at Najá

Although religion still dominates the lives of the Lacandón at Najá, most of their time is taken up with agriculture, hunting, house-building and the other occupations which are necessary for their survival. Settlement patterns have come full circle. In the far distant past the Lacandón lived in villages, but attacks by Spanish forces caused them to scatter and to resettle in small family groups. Now they have taken up community life once again. Their houses, palm-thatched with walls of poles secured by strips of vine, are separated by clearings. Here chickens may be kept, and vegetables grown. But although families live close together there is a great respect for privacy, and visitors would never think of entering a house without first asking permission.

At Najá the Lacandón men still keep their hair long and wear the traditional tunic

Right Chan K'in and his family; *far right* Men of Najá setting off on a hunting trip

Honesty is another prerequisite, and other people's possessions are never tampered with.

Among this northern group there are very few family lineages. Some have adopted surnames in the Spanish style, but Old Chan K'in has kept the totemic name of his ancestors which is '*Max*' or Monkey. Even at eighty he remains active, devoting much of his time to his fields. These lie across the waters of the lake, and instead of walking he often takes his dugout canoe, hollowed out according to Lacandón tradition from one of the great mahogany trees of the forest. The climate round Najá is excellent and land is fertile, capable of producing a wide range of crops. It is customary for each man to select the area he

would like to cultivate. Once he has felled and burned the trees, the land belongs to him alone. Although the Lacandón have lost all knowledge of the complex calendars of the ancient Maya, Chan K'in knows when to sow by watching the seasons and the stars, and by observing the changes in plants and animals. His crops include maize, beans, squash, tomatoes, sweet potatoes, garlic, onions, *chili* and tobacco for the great rolled cigars that the men, women and even children of the group enjoy smoking. Nearer home, in an abandoned maize patch, Chan K'in has fruit trees that produce bananas, limes and lemons, avocado and sometimes mango.

The preparation of food is the duty of Chan K'in's three wives. The tradition of polygamy goes back a long way among the Lacandón, and was a highly practical system when they lived in scattered family groups. Isolated in the depths of the forest, wives could keep one another company while the men were away on hunting expeditions, and share in the work of running the home. In Chan K'in's household the custom persists, and his three wives take turns in pounding out the great *tortillas* of maize. Larger than those eaten among other Indian groups, these are made by shaping the dough on the flat surface of a banana leaf, which rests on a mahogany stool. Apart from this, and a few other stools used as seating, there is little furniture. The Lacandón sleep on platform beds at night, and rest during the day in hammocks that hang from the rafters. These same rafters provide a safe place for storing food and possessions.

Among younger people the custom of polygamy is no longer so successful. Chan K'in's daughter Nuk has been married for ten years to K'in Bor, and has refused to accept a second wife into the home. K'in Bor's ancestry is linked with the Boar, which along with the Monkey is the only other totemic dynasty to survive. Like Chan K'in, K'in Bor takes great care of his fields, but he is also a skilful hunter. In the great lake at Najá fish have become scarce, and game is now a more important source of food than ever, although the animal and bird population is also dwindling fast. Since the introduction of rifles, Lacandón men no longer hunt with their traditional bows and arrows. Each morning before light, K'in Bor sets off with his troop of dogs to scour the forest for parrots, partridges, armadillo and all the other creatures that were once so prolific.

But although hunting and agriculture satisfy day-to-day requirements, the Lacandón are no longer completely self-

sufficient. K'in Bor and many other Lacandón are in touch with the outside world, visiting local towns where they sell bows and arrows and pottery figures to tourists as souvenirs. With their earnings they seek medical treatment, or buy the steel knives, ammunition, petroleum lamps, rice and other commodities that lumberjacks and chicleros introduced among them earlier this century. Modern technology has also provided luxuries like watches and transistor radios which the Lacandón have absorbed into their way of life. The greatest innovation of all, however, must surely be the small Cessna plane which now calls in at Najá. For a lower fare than outsiders would pay, the Lacandón can fly to the nearest town and save themselves several days' walking.

In this way the people of Najá are poised between past and future. As they go about their traditional tasks among the forest trees, they can listen to the music of the town. They can even record their own ceremonies on portable cassette players. The ancient Maya's preoccupation with time has had a strange rebirth in the pride which the menfolk take in their gleaming wristwatches. These and rubber boots contrast strangely with the otherwise timeless appearance of the Lacandón. For although women have taken to wearing gathered skirts of brightly-coloured cloth with their white *huipiles*, and have developed a passion for necklaces of glass beads which they hang with safety pins and coins, the men of Najá have preserved their traditional costume. They still dress in simple tunics, once made from bark cloth but now of white cotton, and let their thick black hair grow down to their shoulders. So although an outsider might be struck by the anachronisms of life among the Lacandón, it would be truer to say that they take from the outside world only what they need and that their roots remain buried firmly in the past.

Religious customs and beliefs provide a strong bond with the ancient Maya, but the Lacandón have more concrete ties with the peoples who once inhabited the great lowland forests of Chiapas. The tall trees that shelter these Indians of today also conceal the stone monuments and ruined temples of their predecessors. In the same way that hunters from both northern and southern groups know intimately the trails and waterways that crisscross parts of the forest, they also know and revere these relics from the past. Small wonder therefore that the Lacandón should have been responsible for the discovery by the outside world in 1946 of one of the most famous of all Maya sites: Bonampak. Two Americans, who had been staying with the southern group by the Lacanjá River, were taken to see the ruins of this ancient centre, which lay not far off, and a few months later a photographer was able to make a second visit with the guidance of these same Lacandón. Soon Mayanists everywhere were to hear about the astounding murals which cover the walls of three vaulted chambers, and which rank among the greatest surviving works of art of ancient Mexico.

Long Count texts have helped archaeologists to date the site to around AD 800, and the murals give us an insight into the magnificence of Maya culture and a greater understanding of life during this period. Although they are obscured by a layer of

Stela from Bonampak, Chiapas
(*c.* AD 800)

stalactite, careful copies made by two artists have recorded
them for posterity. A single narrative unites the murals. In the
first room, high ranking dignitaries wait inside the palace while
the ruler, surrounded by his attendants, is being robed. In the
lower band of the mural there is a group of dancers and
musicians and a procession. The second room shows a battle
between magnificently-costumed warriors and an inferior
tribe. This is followed by the execution and torture of the
captives, while a great lord dressed like a jaguar looks on,
surrounded by his followers. The victory celebrations appear in
the third room, with a procession of dignitaries, a great dance
by lords wearing towering head-dresses of quetzal plumes and
accompanied by musicians, and white-robed ladies drawing
blood from their tongues in voluntary sacrifice.

The People of the Rainforest 143

Copy of a wall painting from Bonampak, showing a battle scene (*c.* AD 800)

These murals show that the Maya were not an entirely peaceful people as has often been thought, but were also a nation of warriors with a highly stratified society. However the murals demonstrate their great artistic ability. The subtlety of the colours combined with the liveliness and realism of the scenes are commemorated in the name of the site, for Bonampak is the Maya word for 'painted walls'.

Some sixty miles away, through dense forest, lies the ceremonial centre of Palenque. It, too, lay hidden from outsiders until it was rediscovered by hardy travellers during the course of the eighteenth century. Then in 1841, when the vogue for lost cities was at its height, a magnificent book appeared. This was *Incidents of Travel in Central America, Mexico, Chiapas and Yucatán*, written by the American author John L.

Late 19th-century excavations of the palace at Palenque

Stephens and illustrated with the meticulous drawings of the Englishman Frederick Catherwood. Together they brought Palenque to the attention of the western world. Stephens described the wildness of the region for his readers:

> The whole country for miles around is covered by a dense forest of gigantic trees, with a growth of brush and underwood

The People of the Rainforest 145

General view of Palenque, in the rainforest of Chiapas, which reached its height *c.* AD 650 (*See also colour plates 9 and 10*)

unknown in the wooded deserts of our own country, and impenetrable in any direction except by cutting a way with a machete. What lies buried in that forest it is impossible to say of my knowledge; without a guide we might have gone within a hundred feet of all the buildings without discovering one of them.

In the middle of desolation and ruin we looked back to the past, cleared away the gloomy forest, and fancied every building perfect, with its terraces and pyramids, its sculptured and painted ornaments, grand, lofty and imposing and overlooking an immense and inhabited plain; we called back to life the strange people who gazed at us in sadness from the walls; pictured them, in fanciful costumes and adorned with plumes of feathers, ascending the terraces of the palace and the steps leading to the temples. . . . In the romance of the world's history nothing ever impressed me more forcibly than the spectacle of this once great and lovely city, overturned, desolate and lost.

Although the site has since been partially cleared by archaeologists, the setting of Palenque remains incomparable. The main group of buildings is surrounded by a chain of low hills, densely covered with tall green trees and sheltering a host of parrots, macaws and howler monkeys. Dominating the central plaza is the Temple of the Inscriptions. This imposing edifice rests on a stepped pyramid sixty-five feet high and is reached by a wide stairway. On the walls of the central chamber and the portico are three panels inscribed with a total of 620 hieroglyphs. These include a number of dates, the latest of which corresponds to the year AD 692.

To the right stands the Palace, with its corbel-vaulted galleries and interior courtyards. Reliefs showing figures, perhaps captives taken in battle or visiting chieftains in a posture of homage, adorn the sides of two of the patios. The builders of Palenque excelled in stucco work, and the galleries are embellished with high-relief stucco decorations of Maya dignitaries carrying the symbols of their authority and accompanied by seated figures. A narrow interior stairway leads up into the four-storey square tower that could have served the inhabitants both as a watchtower and as an observatory.

Various temples are also grouped around the plaza, each standing on a high, stepped platform inset with a frontal stairway. Typical of these temples are the ornate roof combs, and the corbelled archways that were an essential feature of

Maya architecture, both at Palenque and at other sites of the Classic period. The corbel technique consists of superimposing overlapping slabs of stone until the two sides of the room are brought so close together that the gap can be bridged by a single slab. The great weight of these corbelled vaults required extremely thick supporting walls, and it is precisely because of their massive construction that so many Maya buildings have survived. This technique only allowed for narrow rooms, as in the case of these temples, which consist of just two chambers, one inner and one outer. The finely-carved stone slabs that belong to each temple shed some light on their religious context. In the case of the Temple of the Sun, two men who may be priests are shown flanking the mask of a jaguar, here representing the sun in its night-time passage through the underworld. In the Temple of the Cross the same two figures face one another across a symbolic tree of life, and they are portrayed yet again in the Temple of the Foliated Cross, where they appear to be engaged in the worship of a stylised representation of the God of Maize.

Palenque is thought to have been primarily a centre for ceremony, where priests and rulers could work in harmony with the gods to create an ordered society. The pantheon was vast, since every day came under the auspices of a different deity who had to be worshipped and placated. There were also the 'chief gods' representing every aspect of existence. As the carved tablets in the temples show, the Sun God was the object of a major cult. So too was the God of Maize—the plant venerated as the staff of life and deemed to be the gods' highest gift to man.

But although the priests were responsible for winning the favour of the Maize God, it was the simple farmers who had the job of growing the crop. Living in their thatched huts outside the centre, they had to clear the land by felling and burning the trees much as the Lacandón Indians do today, leaving it to lie fallow after only a couple of years' cultivation. Despite their limited range of tools, which amounted to little more than fire-hardened digging sticks, these primitive farmers were able to feed not only themselves but the élite who ruled over them. They also provided the work force necessary for the building of new pyramids, as well as helping to maintain the old.

In return for all this labour, the peasant population would have been watched over by the astonomer-priests whose role it

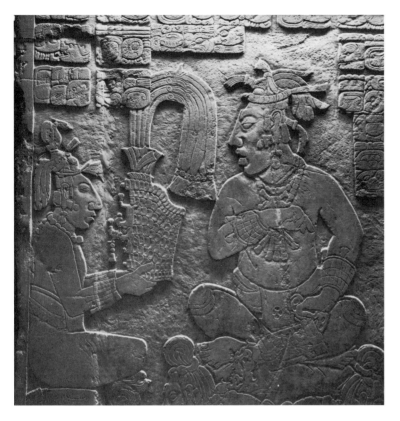

was to satisfy the gods and to control the destiny of the community. The stone buildings of Palenque, with their damp and narrow rooms, might have been uncomfortable as permanent living quarters. But their very smallness conveys an atmosphere of secrecy well suited to meditation and to ritual. The darkness, too, might have been deliberate. Dividing walls partition the rooms, while inner doorways were built out of line with the main entrance as if to shut out the light. This style of architecture, with its heavy corbel-vaulted ceilings, must surely have answered the needs of a priestly class in search of privacy and seclusion to perform their sacred rituals.

Shadowy and anonymous though the priests remain, we now have a direct link with one of the High Lords who ruled over Palenque. This is the result of a unique discovery made by the late Alberto Ruz Lhuillier while he was in charge of excavations at the site. He was standing one day at the top of the Temple of the Inscriptions when he noticed that one of the slabs seemed to have recessed holes for raising it. It proved to be

The Temple of the Inscriptions at Palenque

a trap door, and underneath he found a narrow staircase leading down into the heart of the pyramid. The staircase had been filled in in ancient times with earth and rubble and it took Dr Ruz and his team over two years to clear it. Finally in 1952, at a depth of about sixty ft they reached a stone slab which blocked their way. It was removed, and Dr Ruz entered a great vaulted chamber. In his book on the ancient Maya, he has described these first moments of discovery:

> I found myself in a large crypt that seemed to have been carved from ice—the walls were coated with a gleaming layer of chalk, stalactites hung from the roof like curtains, thick stalagmites rose up from the ground like great candles of wax, all limestone

150 *Of Gods and Men*

formations caused by the seeping of rainwater through the body of the pyramid for more than a thousand years . . . So perfectly constructed was the chamber that the centuries have not affected it, even though it supports the entire weight of the pyramid and the temple.

Dr Ruz went on to observe nine guardian figures in the garb of priests which had been modelled in stucco to adorn the walls. Then his attention was entirely taken up with a great stone sarcophagus that occupied the centre of the chamber. The problem facing him was how to lift off the massive lid, estimated to weigh about five tons. The delicate operation of removing it took twenty-four hours, but at last it revealed a burial chamber containing the skeleton of a Maya chief, decked with jade and surrounded by offerings. Two stucco heads, one on each side of the body, are thought to be likenesses of this great and powerful ruler. Carved on the lid of the sarcophagus is a gigantic reclining figure which may also be a portrait of the deceased.

Glyphs on the side of this stone coffin date the burial to around AD 700, and associated glyphs identify this deified prince and priest as the Lord Pacal. Did he himself plan and order the construction of this great and imposing mausoleum? So exalted was his status that when the crypt had been sealed up, six young men were sacrificed to accompany him to the other world and their bones were left to watch over the entrance. And even though the staircase was then blocked off, a hollow moulding of stucco in the shape of a serpent ran from the sarcophagus to the temple threshold, like a magic link with the outside world. Rediscovered after centuries, the sepulchre of this High Lord who once ruled over Palenque proves that Mexican pyramids could serve not only to support a temple, but also to give lasting glory to the dead.

Unlike the Aztec, the Maya were never a unified people with one capital and one ruler. Their civilisation seems rather to have been based on a loose federation of city states, autonomous but linked by trade and dynastic marriages. On the Yucatán Peninsula, far away from the rainforest sites of Chiapas and Guatemala, there were other important ceremonial centres which flourished around the same time. Among the many cultural traits that the Yucatec shared with the Maya peoples of other areas was a love of fine architecture. This was noted by the Spaniards when they took possession of the region after the Conquest. 'If Yucatán were to gain a name and

Carved stone slab covering the tomb discovered beneath the Temple of the Inscriptions, Palenque

Stucco head found in the burial chamber
in the Temple of the Inscriptions

reputation', wrote Bishop Landa in 1566, 'from the multitide, the grandeur and the beauty of its buildings, as other regions of the Indies have obtained these by gold, silver and riches, its glory would spread like that of Peru and New Spain.'

One of the most remarkable sites in all Yucatán is Uxmal. The peninsula is predominantly flat, but not far from Uxmal are the low hills of Puuc that have given their name to the style of architecture that became popular throughout the surrounding region. Of all the Puuc sites, however, Uxmal is by far the largest and the most splendid. There is still some confusion as to dating, but Long Count glyphs seem to indicate that it was a fully developed centre by the ninth century.

Uxmal is dominated by two great pyramids. One is little more than a ruin, but the other is intact. Spanish friars named this structure 'The Pyramid of the Magician' because of a local

General view of Uxmal, on the Yucatán Peninsula, showing the Temple of the Magician on the right (*see colour plate 11*), and the so-called Nunnery on the left. The site flourished *c.* AD 900

legend which held that the whole edifice had been built in one night by a miracle child! In reality the total period of construction would have been nearer 300 years, because the pyramid is made up of five different structures, each built on top of the last. The most recent temple stands at the summit, 125 ft above ground level, but four earlier ones have been found beneath it.

The Nunnery, a group of buildings in pure Puuc style, was so

Part of the Nunnery at Uxmal

called by the Spaniards, and the totally unsuited name has stuck. The large number of small rooms evidently made them think of a nunnery, but what their real purpose was we do not know. Four complete sets of buildings meet to enclose a quadrangle which is entered by a splendid corbelled archway. The inhabitants of Yucatán had no need to build soaring edifices that would rise above the trees of the rainforest, and they concentrated their energies instead of ornamenting the façades of their buildings. Faced with a thin layer of honey-coloured limestone, the Nunnery features an elaborate display of step-frets and lattice-like designs all achieved with stone mosaics. The gods also provided decorative inspiration. In the

Detail from the façade showing masks of the rain god Chac

dry plains where water is scarce the rain god Chac had risen to prominence, and stylised masks of him, with sky-serpent faces and hooked noses, adorn many of the buildings. John Lloyd Stephens described the quadrangle of the Nunnery as he saw it in the middle of the last century:

> We enter a noble courtyard, with four great façades looking down upon it, each ornamented from one end to the other with the richest, most intricate carving known in the art of the buildings of Uxmal, presenting a scene of strange magnificence surpassing any that is now to be seen among its ruins.

There is a building at Uxmal which has received even greater praise, however. This is the so-called Governor's Palace, often thought to be the single most magnificent building ever erected in the Americas. Set on its own platform mound, it is made up of three interconnecting ranges of rooms which together stretch for over 100 yds. Covering the upper façade is an elaborate mosaic said to include over 20,000 dressed stones which have been set deep into the core of the wall. Lattice-work and step-and-fret ornaments are combined with Chac masks, thatched huts and figures with feathered head-dresses. Like so many travellers who were to come after him, John Lloyd Stephens was amazed at the ingenuity and skill of the builders:

Detail showing a thatched hut from the façade at Uxmal

Away from the region of dreadful rains, and the rank growth of forest which smothers Palenque, it stands with all its walls erect, and almost perfect as when deserted by its inhabitants . . . There is no rudeness or barbarity in the design or proportions; on the contrary, the whole wears an air of architectural symmetry and grandeur; and as the stranger ascends the steps and casts a bewildered eye along its open and desolate doors, it is hard to believe that he sees before him the work of a race in whose eipitaph, as written by historians, they are called ignorant of art, and said to have perished in the rudeness of savage life.

Throughout their long evolution, the Maya were never entirely isolated from the rest of Mexico. Contact with other peoples had been particularly strong at the time of the great civilisation at Teotihuacán, for example, and sherds from Maya bowls have been excavated there, just as Orange Ware from the Mexican Highlands has turned up in the tombs of Tikal. In the tenth century, however, the Maya of Yucatán were to come under the domination of a warlike people who changed the face of their whole culture. These invaders are traditionally supposed to have been the Toltec, who had founded their empire at Tula shortly after AD 900. The open geographic location of the Peninsula left the inhabitants vulnerable to the influence of these invaders from the north, who brought with them a new and agressive militarism, and their own religious cult dedicated to the worship of Quetzalcoatl, the Plumed Serpent.

Signs of the new order are visible at Uxmal, but it was at Chichén Itzá that the Mexican influence was strongest. Formerly called Uucil-abnal or 'Seven Bushes', the site became the Toltec's supreme metropolis, built in the image of Tula. Murals show the violent beginnings of the Toltec era, with scenes of battle and human sacrifice. The social and religious changes that followed the invasion, as Mexican and Maya traditions merged, are reflected in the architecture. Great serpents of stone, processions of stylised warriors and murals reminiscent of those at Tula combine with long-nosed masks of Chac, the Maya rain god. Eagle and Jaguar Knights appear side by side with Maya chiefs in traditional costume.

In this new hydrbid city, the most imposing structure was a great four-sided temple pyramid built in honour of Quetzal-coatl, renamed Kukulcan in Maya. An earlier pyramid discovered beneath it contains a stone jaguar painted red and

General view of Chichén Itzá, showing the merging of Toltec and Maya styles of architecture (*See also colour plates 12 and 13*)

A *chacmool* figure from the Temple of the Warriors at Chichén Itzá, similar to those found at Tula

inlaid with eyes of jade and shell teeth, as well as a reclining figure grasping a receptacle which many archaeologists believe was designed to receive the hearts of sacrificial victims. Known as 'chacmools', these stone sculptures seem to have originated at Tula, and appear in many areas of Chichén Itzá, including the Temple of the Warriors. This majestic building rests on a stepped platform, and faces an impressive grouping of square columns on the north-west side. Carved on all four faces with reliefs of warlike figures, these columns give the building a threatening and militaristic appearance which is reinforced by a line of diminutive Atlantean Toltec warriors supporting an altar within what was once the inner sanctum. Two great feathered serpents flank the entrance to the temple.

Other structures at this splendid but forbidding site include a circular observatory and the Temple of the Jaguars which overlooks a great I-shaped ball court. It is 272 ft long, and the largest in the Americas. Stone rings set high on the sides of the walls prove that the game was played according to Mexican custom, and six reliefs show the decapitation of participants,

Ball court at Chichén Itzá (length 272 feet)

though whether they were victors or losers we cannot be sure. The atmosphere of disciplined violence that hangs over the site is best conveyed by the jaguars and eagles eating human hearts that decorate the facings of two platforms, thought to have been used for staging dances. A third platform stands not far off, its sides entirely covered with carved human skulls impaled on stakes.

The inhabitants of the dry limestone plains of Yucatán relied for their water supply on natural wells called 'cenotes'. At Chichén Itzá there were two such wells. One provided water, but the other was given another purpose—human sacrifice. Bishop Landa described the custom which was still current at the time of the Spanish Conquest:

> Into this well they have had, and then had, the custom of throwing men alive as a sacrifice to the gods, in time of drought, and they believed that they did not die though they never saw them again. They also threw into it a great many other things, like precious stones and things which they prized.

The sacred well has proved a treasure trove for archaeologists, who have recovered a number of gold discs and extremely fine jades from its depths, along with the bones of the sacrificial victims.

The sacred well at Chichén Itzá

By AD 1224 the Toltec appear to have abandoned their great capital, and no further trace of them has been found. Their place was then taken by another warrior group—the Itzá. Their origins remain a mystery, and the Maya spoke of them in unflattering terms, calling them 'tricksters' and 'those who speak our language brokenly'. Scholars have often been confused by the tendency of Maya historical sources to confuse the Itzá with the Toltec. One thing seems certain: the Maya saw each in their turn as a threat to the culture which they had built up over centuries. The ancient chronicles of Chilam Balam evoke the terrors heralded by the new age:

> Then began their reign; then began their rule; then they began to be served. Then those who were to be sacrificed arrived. Then they began to throw them into the well that their prophecy might be heard by their rulers. . . . Then began the introduction of misery there at Chichén Itzá.

While the Toltec and later the Itzá were controlling the Yucatán Peninsula, Maya civilisation in other areas was entering a decline. From the start of the tenth century onwards no more temples were built and the great ceremonial centres were abandoned, left to the encroachment of the surrounding forests. Many reasons have been put forward to explain the collapse of these once-powerful city states—extreme drought, over-exploitation of the land, peasant uprisings and the overthrow of the social system, earthquakes, the spread of some epidemic disease and a foreign invasion from the north. None of these theories have been proven, and the decline of Maya civilisation, like their early beginnings, remains shrouded in mystery.

In the Yucatán, where the Itzá had imposed their stamp on the remnants of Maya and Toltec culture, one last great city was built. This was Mayapán, which became the last stronghold of the Itzá. The region was split by wars, as different Itzá rulers fought for supremacy, and Mayapán was eventually destroyed. It was in this atmosphere of unrest and feudal anarchy that the Spaniards first arrived in 1517. These invaders from across the seas found it harder to subdue the peoples of the Peninsula than the mighty Aztec, because there was no all-powerful leadership which they could crush. By 1541, after many cruel battles with local Indian groups, the Spaniards had gained control of virtually all the territories once held by the Maya, but they were to be faced until the end of their rule with resistance and periodic rebellions.

This lament, from the annals of Chilam Balam, contrasts the new order brought by the Spaniards with the ancient civilisation of the Maya:

Before the coming of the Mighty Men [Spaniards] there was health, devotion; there was no sickness, aching bones, fever or smallpox; no pains in chest or stomach. They walked with their bodies held tall. But the foreigners came and undid everything. They taught fear. They withered the flower, they sucked until they killed the flowers of others so theirs would live. . . . No longer were there priests to teach us. And the second era was established, began to rule, and it was the cause of our death. Without priests, without wisdom, without courage, without shame, everyone the same. There was no longer great wisdom, nor work nor teachings of the lords. The gods that arrived here were worthless! The foreigners came only to castrate the Sun! And the children of their children have stayed with us, and we receive only their bitterness.

The Maya were regrouped in Spanish-style villages, so that they could be kept under control, and in return for their labour they were given religious instruction. The contradictions of the age were epitomised by Diego de Landa, third Bishop of Yucatán. His curiosity about Maya civilisation led him to write a book that was to provide future scholars with invaluable information. But in his determination to crush any vestiges of paganism, he supervised the destruction of 5000 idols, thirteen great stones that had served as altars, 197 vases and twenty-seven rolls of hieroglyphs painted on deerskin. Before the Conquest there must have been thousands of Maya codices, made from bark paper as well as deerskin. These painted manuscripts would have provided a record of astrology and astronomy, history, genealogy, prophecies, rituals and chants. But to date only three have been recovered, one from a waste-paper basket in the National Library of Paris. These, together with a few chronicles transcribed into the Spanish alphabet soon after the Conquest, are all that remain of the literature of the ancient Maya. After the Spanish occupation, the tall trees and thick undergrowth of the forests hid the lowland centres from view, with their stone stelae, their carvings and their murals. And when the outside world began to take a keen interest in these ruins towards the end of the eighteenth century, it was to the Egyptians, Romans, Tartars, Carthaginians or the Lost Tribes of Israel that the credit was given. John Lloyd Stephens and Frederick Catherwood were among the first since Bishop Landa to associate these remains of a once-great culture with the people who still lived in the area.

For the Maya are in no sense a vanished people. Thought to number well over two million, they still occupy the territories of their ancestors. Nearly half this number live in Mexico where there are eight major groupings, each with its own language and traditions, and, although all are Maya, each group is known by a different name. Predominantly a peasant population dependant for their livelihood on agriculture, the present-day Maya have lost all knowledge of the ancient arts and sciences as Chilam Balam had foretold years before. But they have inherited a number of craft skills from their forebears. In the Chiapas Highlands elaborate costumes are still worn, woven on a waist-strap loom and brocaded with a variety of designs. Many of these garments are reminiscent of the styles of dress worn by archaeological figurines from the Island of Jaina and other places. One clay piece from this island even shows a weaver working with her loom.

Trade remains an essential way of life in the Highlands, where various communities specialise in different crafts. Most of the pottery in use throughout the region comes from the village of Amatenango del Valle. The Maya who live here are Tzeltal Indians. Pots are hand-coiled from local clay—a process that is often spread over several days. They are polished with a stone and painted with natural earth colours. Firing takes place in the *patio*, or even out in the muddy roadway. Brightly dressed in colourful clothing, the women from each household gather together to stack the pottery, which is then covered with a mound of wood, cowdung and maize-husks. On a busy day smoke rises up on all sides from the many bonfires that burn throughout the village.

The Tzeltal, like the other Maya groups except the Lacandón,

Potting in the Tzeltal village of Amatenango del Valle. The Tzeltal Indians are one of the many surviving Maya groups.

are nominally Catholics. It is true that in many communities the saints have been identified with the old deities and that pagan beliefs and rituals have been absorbed into the Christian faith. But at the heart of each village stands the church, built by the Spaniards in their fight against what they regarded as idolatry and superstition. Only at Lake Najá, in the depths of the rainforest, are the ancient gods still worshipped.

Among the Lacandón of Najá the god-house has remained the centre of religious activity. Here, in their wall-less temple, with a thatched roof resting on pillars, the Lacandón men come to pray and to make offerings to the gods. Before ceremonies, the sacred conch shell is blown to summon the faithful. Women may not enter, but during long-lasting ceremonies they prepare food for their menfolk in a thatched kitchen built nearby.

The Lacandón worship a great number of gods. The chief deity in times gone by was Kakoch, and he is said to have made the earth, the water, the moon and the first sun. He also made the mayflower, from which the other gods were born. The first to emerge from the flower was Hachakyum, and to him Kakoch made the gift of maize before he himself disappeared. Hachakyum then established order on earth. He built the first home of the gods at Palenque, and from there he moved to Yaxchilán. He made forests, he made stars to illuminate the night, and he made the present sun, because the first one made by Kakoch used to go out every year. Hachakyum also made the Lacandón from clay, and his wife made wives for them. A feud arose between Hachakyum and Kisin, the god of Death, who daubed the new men and women with dark colours. Kisin tried to make human beings of his own, but Hachakyum turned them into animals and they became the soul-counterparts of men. Hachakyum himself created snakes, scorpions and other creatures from the scrapings of clay that were left, while his brother, Akyantho the god of foreigners, made all the domestic animals such as chickens, dogs and pigs which the Spaniards introduced into Mexico. Other gods, which the Lacandón identify with the natural forces that surround them, include K'in the Sun-god, K'ak the lord of Fire, Metzabok the Rain-god, Sukunkyum the ruler of the Underworld and K'ayom god of Song.

Lacandón mythology is very rich and complex, and has many similarities with the sacred book of the Popol Vuh which records the beliefs of the ancient Maya. Both tell of a flood, and both explain that the gods became resentful of the men they had created because they could see everything that happened. Angry with this invasion of their privacy, the gods curtailed their sight, and made them imperfect.

In the temple, the gods are represented by censers with heads. Although prayers may be addressed directly to the god whose favour is needed, the gods are really intercessors with the chief god Hachakyum, and will be asked to pass on all requests and offerings to him. The more serious the request, the more splendid the offerings must be. These can include the burning of incense and black rubber, gifts of food, strips of bark cloth, and balché, which is an alcoholic drink made from the fermented bark of the balché tree. During harvests, in time of sickness or after an excess of rain or sun, old Chan K'in presides over ceremonies in the god-house on behalf of the whole community. While the knobs of copal resin burn in the censers, sending up clouds of perfumed smoke, he waves palm fronds above them and chants his prayers to the gods.

Chan K'in's hopes for the future rest with his two sons, young Chan K'in and K'ayom, and he likes to spend a part of each day teaching them the sacred legends. Sometimes these informal lessons take place in the forest. To the ancient Maya the ceiba tree was the tree of life which sent its roots down into the underworld and reached up into the heavens, and it remains sacred for the Lacandón Indians of today. Seated

Old Chan K'in making offerings in the god house

K'ayom, son of Old Chan K'in, at Najá

beneath its spreading branches, Chan K'in passes on the sacred chants of his people: One of these, The Song of the Jaguar, protects the singer against the jaguars that he may meet in the forest:

> Oh my little brother,
> Don't you know that I sing your song?
> I sing to the markings of your coat.
> Do you hear how I sing to your ears?
> How beautifully marked is your tail.
> You come along the trail,
> Oh my little brother.
> As you come you tear up the earth.
> Don't you know that I sing your song,
> Oh my little brother?

For the Lacandón the forest is both a provider of food and shelter, and also their spiritual home. But since the time of the lumberjacks and the men in search of gum, their way of life has been threatened by a far more serious invasion. The new intruders are Tzeltal Indians, Maya like themselves, but strangers to the ways of the forest. Driven by a need for land, the settlers have been burning large areas of woodland to make way for their maize fields, and upsetting the natural balance by killing off much of the game. The Lacandón are worried about the destruction of their forest, and the threat to their sources of food. Some years ago they applied to the government of Mexico for territorial rights to the land they now occupy, and these have been granted, although there is little that can stop others from settling outside these limits.

Young Chan K'in will have all these problems to deal with in his lifetime. From his father he has learnt the need to protect the environment. Unlike the other Lacandón groups, the people of Najá have agreed not to sell the mahogany trees that grow on their land, because these will be needed by future generations for building, and for the great dugout canoes that are used to cross the lake.

Soon young Chan K'in will also inherit his father's responsibility as religious leader, and old Chan K'in has taken his sons to visit the ancient ceremonial sites. The Lacandón believe that Hachakyum built the first home of the gods at Palenque, and they claim that they have always known about the tomb hidden in the depths of the pyramid. Hachakyum then moved to Yaxchilán, where it is thought that he still lives, together with the other gods. Once the people of Najá went regularly to this ancient centre, to pay their respects to the gods and to seek their favour. Now only a few go, on behalf of the whole community.

It is many days' walk through thick forest to Yaxchilán, although today pilgrims can choose to pool their funds and to pay the pilot from the nearest town to take them by Cessna plane. Once there, the twentieth century recedes again. Growing near the ruined temples, in the shadow of tall trees, are sacred palms, and the Lacandón must gather leaves from them in preparation for their ceremonies. Although there are many gods to be visited in their various houses, it is to Hachakyum that the first offerings are made. His is the main temple, and here before a headless figure of stone the religious

The local Cessna plane calling in at Najá

Offerings and prayers in the House of
Hachakyum at Yaxchilán

rites are held. It is said that when the broken-off head, which stands opposite, rejoins the body, the end of the world will come. The Lacandón bring what they need for the ceremony from Najá, and as the copal resin and the black rubber burn, they chant prayers for themselves, for their families and for everyone at home. The palm leaves, blackened by smoke, will be taken back to Najá as a sign that their prayers have been heard by the gods.

> We are poor and we have suffered.
> This is your ceremony,
> We offer it in your honour.
> We have come to pray to you
> And to weep in your house.
> We have come to speak to you here,
> Here where you live.
>
> We are poor and could not come before.
> This copal resin is for you.
> Here is your payment.
> May the world not end.
> Let our families go on living
> And making tortillas.
> Cure our relatives who are sick
> And could not come.
>
> May the copal incense rise up,
> Copal like a grey cloud,
> Like a perfumed flower.
> Red flowers, flowers of the tree.
> Oh the copal is rising, flying . . .
> Do not sent us harmful things.
> There where we live let no one die.
> Take care of us, we are so few.

* * *

Since the writing of this chapter, there have been a number of changes at Najá. Although old Chan K'in and his followers had previously agreed not to sell the trees on their land, a major lumber company has succeeded in overriding their decision. The directors maintained that, as the other two groups at Lacanjá and Metzabok had both opted to sell their trees, the motion had received a majority vote among the Lacandón. An unpaved road has now been built into Najá by the lumber company, and the felling of an agreed number of trees has begun.

Reactions among the Lacandón have been mixed. A few have left the community, including K'in Bor and his family who have moved to Lacanjá. Meanwhile in Najá, young Chan K'in has learnt to drive a truck, purchased with proceeds from the sale of trees and owned by the community at large. Over recent months, most families have moved their homes to be nearer the road, but although the old god house now stands abandoned, a new one has been erected to take its place. The traditional ceremonies are still held, and so far the signs are that religious faith at Najá continues unabated.

5 The Survivors:
The Christian Compromise

Despite the hardships of the Colonial era and the pressures of the twentieth century, there are still over fifty Indian groups in Mexico, all with their different languages and traditions. Some, like the Maya or the Zapotec, have descended from advanced and powerful civilisations. But others were still semi-nomadic at the time of the Conquest, and the amount of contact which they had with Spanish soldiers and missionaries was largely determined by the remoteness or accessibility of their surroundings. Two such groups with very different histories are the Huichol and the Mayo.

Sheltered by the tall peaks of the Western Sierra Madre, the Huichol are one of the few peoples beside the Lacandón who have managed to cling on to their old religion. Their beliefs and their way of life have changed very little in centuries. But for the Mayo, the outside or non-Indian world is uncomfortably close. They live in the north-west of Mexico, scattered along the Mayo River valley of southern Sonora and the Fuerte River valley of northern Sinaloa, not far from the American border. After the Conquest their low-lying and fertile lands left them vulnerable to attacks by Spanish invaders wishing to settle, and the Mayo opted for an early alliance. Conversion to Christianity soon followed, brought about by Jesuit priests.

Today the Mayo, who number around 30,000, are among the most deeply religious of all Indian peoples. Spanish Catholicism has merged so completely with their ancient beliefs that it is difficult to separate pagan rites from Catholic ritual. Each year the Mayo show their extreme fervour and devotion by acting out the Easter Passion, but they have evolved their own highly personal presentation. Each community performs for itself alone, and everyone is involved.

These unique and complex ceremonies serve as a unifying force among the Mayo, reaffirming their sense of identity which has been under considerable pressure for the last four and a half centuries. Although the Mayo agreed to Spanish domination soon after the Conquest, they later made several bids to regain

Mayo villagers from Bacavachi sharing a communal meal during one of their ceremonies

their freedom. An attempted rebellion in 1740, when they joined forces with the neighbouring Yaqui Indians, was firmly crushed. So too were subsequent revolts, staged during the nineteenth century, when the Mayo and the Yaqui again fought side by side in an attempt to expel all outsiders from their territories. The eventual capture and execution of their leaders in the 1880s ensured the total collapse of the resistance movement among the Mayo.

Their fighting spirit suppressed, they allowed the Mexicans to occupy their land, accepting small plots of ground in compensation. Many went to work for the new landowners on their haciendas, and became peons. Then in 1917 the Mayo took up their weapons yet again, rallying by the thousand to join the revolutionary leader General Obregón. Armed with bows and arrows, they proved their readiness to fight for the new Mexico which, it was widely hoped, would follow the 1910 Revolution and replace the old landholding system. But to their great disillusionment, when the struggle was over, the Mayo found themselves still without the freedom they had been hoping ever since the Conquest to regain. Status as a separate Indian group was denied them, together with any major restitution of their lands.

This deeply felt loss of independence and dignity, together with the gradual disruption of the old native patterns of government, has led the Mayo to channel their energy into religion, the Christianity grafted by the Jesuits on to indigenous Indian beliefs. But Mayo fervour took a direction which the missionaries could not have foreseen. It culminated, around 1890, in a strongly-supported 'prophecy' movement. Their first visionary was a young woman known as Saint Teresa, who claimed to have supernatural healing powers and a knowledge of the future. She predicted a flood which would destroy all Mexicans, but leave the Indians alive, the sole possessors of their ancestral lands. Many of the Mayo began to spread her teachings; and she was succeeded by other prophets, many of whom were deported to the mines of Baja California by the central government which saw them as a threat to civil order. The movement flared up again in the 1960s, when a Mayo seer by the name of Saint Damian told of messages received directly from both God and Jesus Christ. He too warned of a flood, as well as passing on complaints by God about the way the Mayo were being treated, and exhortations not to fail in their religious duties.

Their intense preoccupation with religion has led many outsiders to look upon the Mayo as fanatics. When the Mexican government began its anticlerical campaign in the mid-1920s, the prejudices of local non-Indian peoples led to attacks against the symbols of the Mayo faith. Mayo soldiers, returning to their communities after the revolutionary fighting had ended, found many of their churches sacked or damaged by fire, and their sacred statues, crosses and bells destroyed or stolen. Roughly a decade of religious repression followed, during which large numbers of Mayo fled from Sonora and settled in the neighbouring state of Sinaloa, or took refuge across the border in the United States. When the repression died away, the Mayo were able to regroup once again, and laboriously to rebuild their churches and holy monuments. But the memory of this attack has left a deep scar, and the majority of the Mayo continue to regard non-Indians with profound suspicion.

Despite this mistrust, however, the Mayo are in daily contact with outsiders who control trade and dominate commercial dealings in the area. As a result few villages have succeeded in remaining entirely Indian. Most now have a percentage of Mexican inhabitants who sell them tools and other necessary items, or operate the various systems of transport.

One inevitable consequence of this kind of encroachment by non-Indians is the often bitter land disputes which occur. For the Mayo, their land—and that includes its produce—is sacred. It represents their autonomy as a people, because it is where their ancestors once lived and where they lie buried. Mayo who still own plots of ground, or who have a share in the community-run landholdings called '*ejidos*', follow tradition by planting maize, squash and beans, occasionally combining these with more recently introduced crops such as barley, wheat, cotton or sesame seed. When family needs have been met, the excess produce is sold. Along the sandy coastline, the sea provides fish and salt deposits, offering the Indians who live there an alternative source of both food and income.

But times are changing. The non-progressive style of farming still favoured by the Mayo is in marked contrast with the modern methods which are in use on the vast neighbouring Mexican landholdings. Sonora and Sinaloa are prosperous states, committed to constant economic expansion, and over the last two decades the face of the land has altered dramatically. With the country's economy geared to optimum agricultural production, local landowners and corporations assume the right to cultivate the area freely in the national interest. Careful irrigation has transformed the land: well-kept fields spread out across the river valleys, taking in land once farmed by the Indians. Enormous tracts of native forest, which have traditionally provided the Mayo with building materials, firewood, game, wild fruits and medicinal herbs, are being cleared to make room for large-scale farming projects, often aimed at an international market. As in the past, it is the Mayo who make up a large part of the labour force required to keep such projects going, and the vast crops of cotton, cereals, oil grains, fruit and vegetables are harvested by the landless and by smallholders who cannot live entirely off their own land.

And so, despite their misgivings, the Mayo have been drawn into the national economic system, and close contact with the Mexican way of life has over the years led them to adopt many of its characteristics. The village of Bacavachi is typical. Situated in the Mayo River valley, it is the home of approximately 400 Indians. Although, unlike most Mayo villages, it has attracted relatively few outsiders, the fusion of Indian and Mexican cultures is immediately visible. Traditional in style, the majority of houses are *adobe*-built and windowless. They usually consist of a single room, with a cooking area outside the door, and nearly all have an *adobe* oven in the yard where bread

is baked. But few other Mayo skills—even ones of a generation ago—have been kept up. Locally-fired pottery and the thick, woollen blankets, woven on semi-vertical looms, which were once important features of Mayo life, have been largely replaced by factory items made from plastic, aluminium and synthetic fibres. Their dress has for a very long time been no different from that of the average rural Mexican.

The process of assimilation which the villagers of Bacavachi have undergone is reflected in other ways too. Time spent working on local agricultural holdings, together with visits to the nearby town to seek medical treatment and legal advice, or to shop, keep them in constant touch with the world around them and, in common with other Mayo, they take a keen interest in politics. Self-government as an ethnic group is out of their reach, but they make full use of their votes at election time, supporting the candidate whose policies seem most likely to answer their needs. Older members of the community recall with pride how, back in the 1930s, the State of Sonora had a Mayo governor. Education is highly valued in the village, for it offers the younger generation a chance to improve their position, and on the whole the state-run school is well attended. Few adults in Bacavachi have had more than a couple of years' schooling, which limits their role in Mexican society to that of poorly paid labourers and unskilled manual workers. But many hope that, with the benefits of education, their children will be

The Christian Compromise 175

able to compete for better jobs on an equal footing with non-Indians.

Although villagers recognise the values of the non-Indian world, with the emphasis upon wealth and personal advancement, they have not adopted them wholesale. United by their traditions and beliefs, they have retained a strong sense of loyalty, not only to their own community, where family ties and respect for the elderly are still prime considerations, but to their race as a whole. Although Spanish has been widely learnt, large numbers of Mayo—or, as they call themselves, 'Yoremem'—still speak their own language. To outsiders the language is 'Cahita'—a misnomer, like so many other names applied to the Indians by the Spaniards. The legend goes that Jesuit missionaries asked the Indians what language they were speaking. Mistaking the question, they replied: 'Cahita', which translated means 'nothing'. To the Mayo no term could be a less accurate description, for 'Yoremnok' (to use their own word) serves both as a private language when they are in the company of Mexicans, and also links them with their past, enabling them to convey thoughts and emotions that are essentially Indian.

Dominating these thoughts and emotions, now as in times gone by, is religion. So many aspects of Mayo life have been undermined, but despite past persecution their religious faith remains unshaken, ensuring their autonomy as a people and making up for their sense of deprivation and lack of status in the outside world. The Mayo respond to gibes of 'fanaticism' from non-Indians by regarding their critics as irreligious, by condemning as ignoble the pursuit of riches and the accumulation of material possessions, and by advocating self-sacrifice and poverty as the virtues to be admired and emulated. For the villagers of Bacavachi, their chief duty lies in serving God and the Saints. Their church, rebuilt with bricks and mortar after the attacks of the 1920s, inspires great pride, and its upkeep is the responsibility of the whole community.

Although Jesuit teachings erased conscious memories of the old religion, many pre-Conquest beliefs have lingered on. God and the Saints in Mayo tradition have strong links with past deities who embodied the forces of nature. God has taken on the attributes of the Sun, and the Virgin Mary those of the Moon. This synthesis of Christian and pagan can most clearly be seen in the calendar festivals of the Catholic church, which mark the

high point of village life. To take part in such celebrations is to be truly Mayo, but participation is very demanding, both in terms of time and financial cost. Of these celebrations, the most important and the most demanding is without doubt the Easter Passion.

Day by day, over the Easter period, the Bible story is acted out, culminating in the crucifixion and resurrection of Christ. For the villagers this is a highly emotional ordeal, as one participant's words reveal:

> We have been carrying out these ceremonies ever since our ancestors began this religion. We are Catholics, and we do the best we can to carry on the tradition. Since I was born, over seventy years ago, I have been present at this feast. As a child I took part, and even at my age I am still taking part. Each year, during Easter week, we re-enact what happened long ago when the Jews crucified Christ. He gave his life for us to save humanity. If he had not, there would have been no humanity — it could not have existed. When we see the crucifixion we grieve for Mary, Our Mother. And although we feel great joy once Christ has risen, it is mixed with a terrible sadness that weighs upon us. But you see, this is our religion and we have no choice.

What comes across from such remarks is the extreme pride villagers take, not only in being Catholic, but in having what they feel is an accurate knowledge of Bible history. And even though a few non-Christian Mayo legends have crept into the story, this knowledge is impressive—especially when one considers that Bacavachi has no priest, either resident or visiting. One reason for this is the smallness of the community, although another may be the antagonism that has existed between Mayo Indians and clergy ever since the religious suppression of the 1920s. There has been a strong tendency among the Mayo to hold the clergy responsible, and to blame the greed of individual priests for the wave of anticlerical feeling that brought about the attacks. The priests, on the other hand, are critical of the many unorthodox features of Mayo worship and ritual, often preferring to remain with their Mexican followers.

The villagers do not lack spiritual guidance, however, for they have their own religious leaders in whom they place complete trust. Elected for their knowledge of Catholic prayers, Bible lore and ceremonial procedure, they take care of the church, administer its funds, and help with the organisation of festivals. At the head of the religious hierarchy is Benacio Gomez, the 'temasti' or sacristan. His is a life of total dedication; during the course of a year he may spend anything up to two hundred days, and even nights, engaged in ceremonies and vigils. But the satisfaction he feels is sufficient reward:

> Here in Bacavachi we are still carrying on the traditions which our ancestors left for us. Although our superiors are dead, we have inherited their instructions and their teachings, which are in accordance with those of the priests. I learnt what I know from my superiors, and it is my duty to teach those who will come after me.

Throughout the Easter Passion, the authority and guidance of the sacristan are crucial at every stage, but the organisation of events depends also upon a complex network of fraternities. These fraternities, with their different ranks and strict codes of behaviour, appear to have combined the Jesuit talent for organisation with the more ancient Mayo systems of military and civil government. Leaders are elected by the members, and serve for as long as they are asked. Members are recruited by means of a ritual contract or 'manda' with a saint. If the saint grants the favour requested, which most often lies in curing diseases and injuries, then the supplicant must fulfil his or her promise and serve a term, usually amounting to three years, with the appropriate group.

Benacio Gomez, the *temasti* or sacristan, administering holy water

In addition to the various church groupings that come directly under the authority of the sacristan, there are three main fraternities, each with its own clearly defined role. The order of the 'Pariserom' is by far the largest group, with a nucleus of fifty-two young men, and it is made up of Pilates who represent the Governor Pontius Pilate and of Pharisees. During festivities, members act the part of the Jews and pursue, capture and crucify Jesus. Equally important are the 'Paskome' or ceremonial hosts. The men and women who

A group of Pharisees, the tormentors of Christ (*see also colour plate 35*)

belong to this organisation have bound themselves to provide food and hospitality for the duration of the feast to all who take part. The financial liability involved is great, even allowing for the contributions of other villagers. Few members can afford to serve the three years of their term consecutively. The Paskome are also responsible for engaging the 'Paskola' dancers to perform. These dancers are members of the third grouping: the Confradia del Culto de los Montes, or the Fraternity of the Cult of the Mountains, whose traditions are closely linked with the pagan past of the Mayo. Status within the fraternities brings considerable honour and respect. The fact that both of these are hard to win in the world outside Bacavachi serves in turn to reinforce the power and importance of the fraternities.

Preparations begin long before the actual celebrations. The church is cleaned by members of the community, and the surrounding area is marked out with fourteen crosses, each decorated with green branches, to represent the Stations of the Cross. In the meantime, the Paskome begin their rounds of the village to collect donations of food and money. These supplement their own enormous contribution, which may be equivalent in monetary terms to one man's yearly earnings. Staple foods are grown locally, but luxury items must be bought from outside traders. Transport has to be organised, and further obligations include the ordering of fireworks and the building of a temporary cooking area.

Temporary cooking area, where coffee is being served to the Three Marys

Preliminary ceremonies begin as early as Ash Wednesday, and on the following Friday the Pharisees and the Pilates initiate their evil rule in Bacavachi: only after the Resurrection will divine order reassert itself. Both groups present a malevolent and threatening appearance, in keeping with the roles they play. The Pilates are the leaders. Dressed entirely in black, their faces hidden by black drapes and masks of white cardboard, they have about them an air that is both sinister and dramatic, intensified by the pointed lances which they carry, and by the way they tower above the rest—for they alone ride horses during festivities. The costumes worn by the Pharisees, or foot-soldiers, strike a more humorous note. Their heads and shoulders are covered with hairy masks of goatskin, shaved in parts and whitened so that features can be painted on to simulate animal or human faces. Wooden noses, ears and lips are nailed on, heightening the grotesque effect. Clothing consists of trousers, worn under a long blanket with an opening for the head; and completing the costume is a jingling belt hung with metallic cartridges. These have replaced the deer hooves which were used until recently, a legacy from earlier times when the Mayo were hunters rather than farmers. One very ancient feature that has survived is the strings of butterfly cocoons filled with tiny pebbles, which are tied round the ankles and rattle with the slightest movement.

It is difficult to establish how such costumes evolved, although there is no doubt that they are the result of a fusion between Indian and post-Conquest elements. Perhaps the Mayo were inspired by early biblical illustrations of the exotic styles of dress attributed to the Jews. Few explanations are to be had from the villagers themselves, who only know that these costumes are worn 'because it is the custom'. Further attempts to gain information can give rise to humorous misunderstandings. One Pharisee, asked during festivities if goatskin masks had been worn for a long time in Bacavachi, replied

Mounted Pilatos, followers of Pontius Pilate (*see also colour plate 36*)

helpfully: 'Oh no, we just put them on this morning!' Like the costumes, the events too reveal a mixture of pagan and Catholic tradition. In common with so many other Indian groups in Mexico, the Mayo were greatly drawn to the processions and the pomp that characterised the Catholic church of the sixteenth century, at the same time retaining a number of their own rituals.

Palm Sunday marks the start of Holy Week, and from this time onwards ceremonies take up the greater part of each day, demanding the participation of everyone in the village. Overshadowing most other events on Palm Sunday is the

Jesus Christ, in glasses and blue denim, is put on trial by the Pharisees

nomination of the old man who is to represent Christ. Chosen as the man most respected by the community, he is brutally taken from his home by the Pariserom. Over the next few days he is paraded from house to house by his captors as they raise money to cover their costs. As well as an unblemished reputation, Christ's representative must possess great physical stamina, for during his term he will have to undergo a number of all-night vigils, and also withstand the aggression of his enemies.

Hostilities reach their peak on Easter Thursday. After an enactment inside the church of the Last Supper, followed by the betrayal of Judas, the old man is once again taken prisoner by the Pariserom and led out to the great cross which faces the doorway. A strangely anachronistic yet dignified figure, wearing blue jeans and a denim jacket, he listens impassively as the sacristan uses a mixture of Mayo and Spanish to explain the charges which are being brought against him. Pronounced guilty, the old man is dressed in a white cotton kilt suggestive of a loincloth, and a brightly printed kerchief is tied round his head to symbolise the crown of thorns which Jesus wore.

No sooner has this mock trial ended, than the Pariserom begin to chase the old man around the fourteen Stations of the Cross, subjecting him to repeated indignities and even knocking him to the ground. This ritual, ostensibly performed to illustrate the Bible story, is an undoubted survival from an earlier

The Three Marys preparing to defend Christ as he is chased round the Stations of the Cross.

hunting ceremony. During the chase, which happens at great speed, Jesus is defended by his spiritual guardians, the Paskome, and the Three Marys, who have also taken a special vow to participate in the Easter Passion. Dressed in white like brides, these girls represent the Virgin Mary, Mary Magdalene and Mary Dolores. It is their sacred duty to offer the old man water, to support him when he stumbles and to beat off the Pariserom whenever possible.

To an outsider Christ's captors might seem a disorderly mob, taking advantage of their disguises and their roles to indulge in an excess of buffoonery and aggression, as they persecute the old man and mock everything the Mayo hold sacred. But this assumption would be far from the truth. Despite their simulated

indiscipline, the Pariserom are in fact responsible for keeping order during these Easter rituals, punishing any villager who misbehaves. They themselves are bound by a strict code of conduct, which is enforced by their captain, who wears no costume. Middle-aged, with many years of faithful service behind him, he watches to see that the young men under his command discharge their religious obligations to the community. Chief among these is the vow of silence that each Pharisee takes before celebrations begin, and which is binding until his loss of power at the moment of the Resurrection. Denied any form of speech, the Pariserom resort to mimicry: they go through the motions of defecation and sexual intercourse, and show disrespect to the old, deliberately flouting

The Christian Compromise 185

the normal Mayo code. They also parody devout onlookers as they mourn Christ's suffering. Prayers are disrupted by the jingling of their belts, and by the sound of the drums which various members of the fraternity are allowed to carry as a sign of rank. Yet in spite of their bawdy behaviour during festivities, many keep the cross of a rosary in their mouths to remind them of their sacred objectives.

Close behind the Pariserom, as they chase their captive round the Via-Crucis, come the villagers. With horror and anguish they witness the sufferings of Jesus, and their emotions are none the less sincere because they are taking part in an event that is re-enacted yearly. Octavio Paz, the Mexican writer and poet, has described the deep devotion to Christ that Indian people feel—a devotion which could almost be said to go deeper than that inspired by God the Father. Paz explains it by suggesting that the Indians of modern Mexico are able to identify with Christ because, although he was a Redeemer, he was also a victim: 'The Mexican venerates a bleeding and humiliated Christ, a Christ who has been beaten by the soldiers and condemned by the judges, for he sees in him a transfigured image of his own identity.' These words, taken from 'The Labyrinth of Solitude', were written by Paz in the general context of Mexico. Applied to the Mayo, they perfectly describe the emotional response to Christ which is shared by all those who participate in the Easter Passion, and it is on a note of deep sorrow that Thursday ends. Many villagers will even stay up all night in preparation for Good Friday—the saddest day of the year.

By the early hours of Friday morning, mourners have already begun to gather in the church to pray, and to pay their respects to the dead Christ. Among the Mayo the crucifixion is mimed. It is also symbolised by an empty coffin and by the cross with its image of Jesus. On one side of the crucified figure is fixed the sponge of vinegar that touched his lips, and on the other the spear that pierced his side. Both the coffin and the cross are placed near the altar, where they remain while the sacristan holds a service. When the time comes for the great procession, they are carried outside. Behind the cross walks the old man who has been standing in for Jesus, and he is followed by the coffin-bearers. All the church guilds are present, and each member keeps the position in the cortège that corresponds to his or her rank. Last come the villagers, who are dressed as for a

funeral. Although black is only worn today by older women, all the women have shawls over their heads.

As the sombre procession visits the Stations of the Cross, a steady chanting is kept up, with a long stop at each Station for prayers. These are led by the sacristan, who keeps to a simplified version of the Catholic litany which he intones in both Spanish and Latin. Helping him is a special guild made up entirely of women, the standard-bearers. Their flags fluttering, they kneel with him at each cross and chant the responses. Despite the solemnity of the occasion, the Pariserom never cease their clowning: they ridicule the mourners and tease the small boys and girls who belong to the two children's orders. 'The Brides of

The standard bearers

The Christian Compromise 187

The children's order of the 'Brides of Christ' inside the church

Christ', dressed in white, form the female group, while the boys, who wear black suits, are known as the 'Kings' or the 'Angels'. Together they represent the forces of good that must ultimately triumph. But for the villagers, as they follow the coffin along the Via-Crucis on its symbolic journey to the tomb, there is no thought of tomorrow's Resurrection, for the enemies of Christ are still in control. Ceremonies end back in the church, the final resting place of the coffin, where the sacristan and a few faithful

The downfall of the Pharisees: their masks are piled up in front of the cross ready for burning

followers will hold a night-long vigil.

Early on Saturday morning, the grief that has possessed the village is dispelled by the clanging of the great bell that hangs beneath the main cross in the church patio. Traditionally silent during the period of mourning, its sound tells villagers that Christ has risen. Soon the surrounding area is full of people, eager to celebrate the Resurrection. Christ's victory heralds the downfall of the Pariserom, and as the hour of noon approaches they prepare to renounce their power in a series of complicated rituals in which Christian and pagan beliefs are inextricably mixed. Accompanied by the noise of rockets and the tolling of the bell, the masked Pharisees run three times, at great speed, between the cross and the church. Their rule is now ended, and they sink exhausted to the ground where they wait for the help that only their godparents can give them. These are men and women who are bound by a vow to give both financial and spiritual support to the Pariserom throughout the three years of their service. Now their participation is required, for their godsons are relying on them to relieve them of their masks and the other symbols of their evil past, and to help them regain their status as men.

Shielded by their godparents from the gaze of onlookers, the Pariserom undergo what amounts to an exorcism from the malevolent forces that have possessed them. Gasping for breath they make the sign of the cross: it is worth remembering that the cross is also the immemorial Indian symbol of the four cardinal points. What follows is regarded as a baptism, marking the rebirth of each Pharisee as a man. The first purification rite is with air, as the young men are fanned by their godparents. The second involves water: passing along the lines of crouched figures, the sacristan sprinkles each youth with holy water, thereby bringing him even nearer to a state of grace. Purification by fire is the last and the most spectacular part of the baptism. Near the church a large bonfire has been lit. After the masks and the other paraphernalia belonging to the Pharisees have been collected up, they are hurled on to the fire where they are consumed by the flames. God, identified by the Mayo with the Sun, has symbolically burned the enemies of Christ, and their rebirth as men is complete.

Divine order has returned at last to Bacavachi, and this is the cue for the Paskola dancers to begin their own celebrations and so round off the events of Holy Week. The villagers form a tight circle to watch them perform. An aura of mystery surrounds these dancers, because they represent the forces of nature and the supernatural. As members of the Fraternity of the Cult of the Mountains, they are believed to be in close contact with the world of the forest, and in particular with the spirit of the mountains, who is said to be their guardian. Described by many as a little old man with a white beard, he watches over them and gives them their skill as performers. The Paskola are the

only participants who are paid to take part.

The Paskola costume is a strange mixture of ancient and modern. It includes leather sandals, a spotless white T-shirt, and a length of white cotton cloth which is brought between the legs and then wrapped around them to serve as kneelength trousers. Holding up this primitive garment is a leather belt hung with small round bells, and wound round the ankles are long strings of butterfly cocoons filled with tiny pebbles like those worn by the Pharisees. The noise of the cocoons and the jingling of bells reinforce the rhythms of the dance. So too does the wooden rattle mounted with metal discs that each performer carries, beating it with the right hand against the open palm of the left. The accompanying music is provided alternately by two separate sets of instruments. The first consists of the pre-Conquest flute and drum; the second of the fiddle and the harp which the Spaniards introduced into Mexico from Europe. Dressed in their everyday clothes, with the addition of a large paper flower pinned to their palm hats, the musicians remain seated in a corner of the dancing area and alternate between these two styles of music.

In Bacavachi the chief Paskola performer is also a maskmaker, responsible for carving the wooden masks that he and the other dancers wear. These unique black, white and red masks, incised with decorative symbols and human features, are fitted with eyebrows and beards of white horsehair. During the music of the harp and violin, performers wear the mask

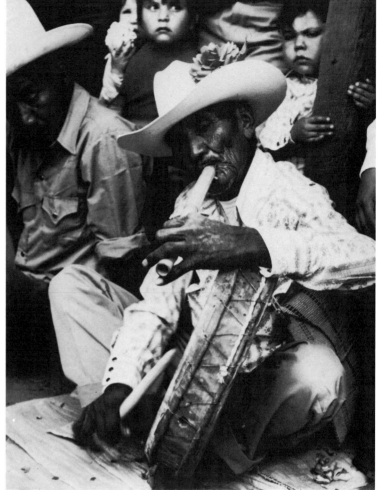

pushed to the back of the head. When it is the turn of the flute and drum, it is brought forward to cover the face. Not even Lupe Valdez, the chief performer, can explain why this is done, but one reason would seem to be that the more ancient music demands the traditional use of the mask. The steps, which require great agility and years of practice, seem to display no European influence whatsoever, and although each of the four dancers performs singly, they seem to vie with one another for supremacy. The head, topped with a large paper flower, is bent forward to follow the line of the torso, and with springy steps the dancer responds to the changing rhythms set by the musicians. The footwork is highly complicated, and the body

movements have about them a primitive quality that suggests
the wild animals of the forest. In most villages the Paskola are
joined by a dancer impersonating a deer. He wears a deer's
dried head, and his movements, as he leaps and bucks,
occasionally pausing as if to scent the wind, are directly
inspired by the deer.

While the dancing continues, the Paskome fulfil their
promise to feed the community. In the cooking area great
cauldrons of sweet coffee and meat stew are put to simmer over
an open fire, and throughout the rest of the day all those who
have taken part in the Passion will be invited to sit down at the
trestle tables to eat and drink. Offers of payment are never

The Christian Compromise 193

made, for they would contravene the terms of the vow and offend the Paskome. Communal meals are one of the most important aspects of the Easter festivities, because they draw people together in an atmosphere of harmony and goodwill. Villagers like to think of themselves as a unit, rather like a large family, and the sharing of food enforces this feeling.

This sense of autonomy is particularly sought after by those who have taken leave of absence from jobs in other places, and have returned to Bacavachi to be present during Holy Week. Even as onlookers, they are fulfilling a religious duty and strengthening their ties with the community. The Easter Passion allows the Mayo to give free rein to their creativity, and to reaffirm their Indian identity. The villagers of Bacavachi are lucky in that they are able to celebrate Easter in relative privacy, with no tourists and few outsiders. In many other villages and towns, where there is a large non-Indian population, the Mayo have only a small area where they can perform their rituals. They are hemmed in by jostling and exuberant crowds, while the music of their dances and the sound of their prayers are drowned by the hubbub of the beer-tents and travelling fun-fairs which are there for the amusement of the Mexicans. Such commercialism is repellent to the Mayo, who view the Passion with deep solemnity as a time of intense sadness and joy, which has nothing to do with selling beer and having a good time.

In Bacavachi celebrations will last right through Sunday, with more dancing by the Paskola, more feasting at the expense of the Paskome, and yet another procession to symbolise the joyous meeting between Mary and Jesus, each represented by their image from the church. Vast sums of money will have been spent, the savings from many months' hard work. Outsiders tend to criticise the Mayo for what they see as an improvident and feckless way of life, but for the villagers of Bacavachi the time and money spent on these celebrations bring a deep satisfaction. At the end of Holy Week, they are secure in the knowledge that their ceremonies have kept the world in a state of balance and harmony for another year, and that the forces of virtue have once more triumphed over evil.

6 The Survivors:
The Way of the Ancestors

In order to protect their Indian identity, the Mayo have had to adapt to a non-Indian way of life, embracing the Catholic religion with a fervour which few other groups can match. By contrast, the Huichol have made few concessions to Spanish or Mexican influences. More than four and a half centuries after the Conquest they are still carrying on the traditions and beliefs of their ancestors. Their mythology and their rituals have remained largely untouched by Christianity, but hark back to ancient times when the Huichol were still semi-nomadic, living not through agriculture but as hunters and gatherers.

Cut off from the outside world by the mountain peaks and deep canyons of the Western Sierra Madre, the Huichol live in one of the most remote and rugged parts of Mexico. This region, which covers just over 1000 square miles, stretches into the states of Jalisco, Nayarit, Durango and Zacatecas. During the rainy season the terrain becomes virtually impassable, while at other times of the year a plane ride, or a journey on foot or horseback lasting several days, is necessary to reach even the least remote of the Indian settlements. Although census-taking in such an area has proved unreliable, the Huichol are at present believed to number over 10,000. United by a common language related to that of the Aztec, they refer to themselves as the '*Wixarika*', roughly translatable as 'prophets' or 'healers'.

It was their inhospitable surroundings that saved the Huichol from invasion at the time of the Conquest. A history of the region, written soon afterwards by a Jesuit priest, Father Ortega, included the following description: 'It is so wild and frightful to behold that its ruggedness, even more than the arrows of its warlike inhabitants, took away the courage of the conquerors; because not only did the ridges and valleys appear inaccessible, but the extended range of towering mountain peaks confused even the eye.' Not until well into the eighteenth century did troops finally succeed in penetrating the area.

However, although nominally conquered, the Huichol

Huichol territory, high in the Sierra
Madre

continued to oppose Spanish domination, and as late as 1894 another visitor to the region, the Norwegian anthropologist Carl Lumholtz, was told by the Governor of Jalisco: 'You will find in a corner of the state absolute savages who wear their hair long, and refuse to pay taxes to the government. Once in a while they come here to see me and sleep in the courtyard of the Palacio, which they seem to consider as their house.' It is their pride, linked with a refusal to be influenced by outsiders, that has enabled the Huichol to keep their culture virtually intact. Lumholtz, who was the first non-Huichol to live with the group, and who documented their way of life in the 1890s, wrote of them: 'Their self-esteem is equal to anyone's. Never for a moment will a Huichol allow that any other race may be superior to his own. Even when far from home among the whites, the Huichol will bear themselves as if they had never known masters.'

196 *Of Gods and Men*

Eighty years on, the Huichol still take the same pride in their heritage. While other Indian groups may admire and even envy city people, the Huichol are awed by nothing and no one. It is true that they have adopted such Spanish importations as steel knives or cattle, and many buy transistor radios. But these are innovations that can be integrated into daily life without altering its basic structure, and the Huichol sense of their own dignity remains unshaken. Outsiders are looked on with mistrust, and marriage with them is shunned, for it is believed to entail the loss of Huichol identity and to bring severe punishment on the culprit after death.

In the past, relations with neighbouring landowners have often been violent because of the encroachment on Huichol lands. Even today relations are strained, for, although the Huichol have legal tenure of their zone, the land disputes continue. Nearly forty per cent of the population speak no Spanish at all, which makes matters worse, and like many other Indian groups they are further hampered in their dealings with outsiders by illiteracy and by their inability to understand legal documents. But the Huichol refuse to feel humbled or oppressed, preferring whenever possible to hold themselves aloof in the fastness of the Sierra, and to acknowledge only their own laws.

Huichol society is highly ordered. The territory is divided into five areas, each with its own administrative centre, where the Huichol officials live. Elected yearly by a council of elders who represent the wisdom and experience of the group, officials are expected to dispense justice and to reach decisions on political, social or ceremonial matters. The bulk of the population lives in remote settlements, however, several hours or even several days walking distance apart, and because of this isolation inhabitants rely for day-to-day guidance on the judgement and advice of an elder from within the community.

These small settlements, known in Spanish as *ranchos*, are generally held together by family ties, and number around twelve households. Built of stone, *adobe* or wattle, Huichol homes are usually rectangular, although in the past they were more often round or even hexagonal. With their thatched roofs of palm, leaves or grass, they blend into the rugged landscape. Because of the difficulties of the terrain, living patterns are determined by water-holes, and also by the availability of fertile land, which is scarce. Held in common, it reverts to the

Traditional Huichol house with a thatched roof

community as soon as an individual ceases to cultivate his share, and when the soil becomes depleted settlers may be forced to move, clearing forested areas with axes or *machetes* and by burning.

The Huichol year consists of a dry and a wet season. In June, when the earth is soft after the rains, seeds are planted with the help of a digging stick, most fields being too steep to take any form of plough. Crops are harvested in November. Like other Mexican Indians, the Huichol depend for their livelihood on maize, beans and squash which are grown together on the same plot of land. In the deeper valleys, where the climate is semi-tropical, cucumber, chili, tobacco, sugarcane, sweet potatoes, watermelon and bananas may be grown, but these are luxuries. In an attempt to supplement their often meagre diet, the Huichol sometimes gather wild fruits and vegetables, or go on fishing expeditions to the Chapalanga river and its tributaries that flow through their territory. Meat is rarely eaten, because wild game has become scarce, and domestic animals are killed on ceremonial occasions only. Throughout the region, food production is at a minimum subsistence level, and during much of the year the Huichol face hunger and malnutrition. On occasion communities may even be driven to consume the whole year's crop, leaving no seeds for next year's planting.

But among the Huichol, physical hardships are balanced by

an intense spiritual awareness. Their technology may be rudimentary, but the Huichol world vision is extremely complex. Material privations are looked on with indifference, for despite their poverty the Huichol feel rich in their *'kupuri'*, roughly translatable as 'soul', and they are sustained by an unshakeable faith in the meaningfulness of life. From the cradle to the grave it is invested with a symbolism which it is often hard for an outsider to interpret. Most Huichol religious belief defies rational explanation, and indeed in their case the very word religion may be misleading. The Huichol regard religious belief as a highly personal matter, which reaches far beyond the confines of any formalised institution. Thus religion is inextricably bound up with life itself, and distinctions are never made between the sacred and the profane. Christianity, introduced into the area during the eighteenth century by Franciscan missionaries, made little impact, and Lumholtz was moved to write at the end of his stay with them in the 1890s: 'In spite of missionary work in the past, today there is no priest among them, the churches are in ruins, and the Huichol are living in the same state of barbarism as they were when Cortés first put foot on Mexican soil.'

In the 1950s, Franciscan missionaries renewed their attempts to bring Christianity to the region, but the overall situation has changed little since the time of Lumholtz. The Huichol continue to serve their many gods—so many, indeed, that there is probably no single individual who could name them all. For the Huichol everything is alive, and therefore divine. Plants, like human beings, have souls: otherwise they could not grow. Yet the Huichol have no term in their language which corresponds to the word 'gods', and concepts such as 'prayer' or 'worship' are equally alien.

In no sense remote beings, the Huichol deities are the forces of nature that surround them in their everyday lives. Looked on with awe, but also with affection, they are known by terms of close kinship such as Grandfather, Father or Mother. If pleased, they will grant food, health and life itself, but if neglected they may become angry, withholding rain and sending famine, misfortune and disease. For the Huichol the happiness and beauty of their existence lie in feeling themselves to be in harmony with the natural world, and in order to win the protection and goodwill of their gods they make them offerings, vows and sacrifices, at the same time drawing strength from this day-to-day contact with the divine.

The landscape itself is sacred, dotted with rocks, hills and springs which are regarded as gods in their own right, and the Huichol make pilgrimages to visit them, often journeying far outside their territories to the Pacific Ocean in the west, or to the state of San Luis Potosí in the north. Among the most important of these natural shrines are the caves and underground springs that lie near the ceremonial centre of Santa Catarina, in the heart of the Huichol mountains. Pilgrims go there to bathe in the holy water, and to leave flowers and other gifts for the deities who inhabit the cave. Stories are told of angry priests in the last century who tried to destroy the strangely-shaped boulders that are found there. They little realised that their zeal to abolish idolatry, if carried out to its logical conclusion, would have meant the destruction of the entire landscape; for to the Huichol it is all sacred.

But whereas these deities are often of local importance only, the God of Fire is revered throughout the entire region. Thought of as the oldest deity, 'Grandfather Fire' is the special protector of the Huichol, and in the earliest times it was he who taught them how to please the other gods. Today he continues to watch over them, for it is fire that clears their fields for planting, lights up the darkness, provides warmth, and cooks their food. As a result he is regarded with grateful affection, and when Huichol travellers see fire being used outside their territories,

Huichol men in their everyday costume preparing palm for thatching

they tend to greet him like a friend who is also on a visit to the outside world.

In common with the Aztec and many other peoples of pre-Conquest Mexico, the Huichol hold the sun in great awe. Although born in ancient times to light and warm the earth by day as 'Grandfather Fire' did by night, 'Father Sun' is not such a benevolent deity. He is the source of many illnesses, as well as of drought, and the Huichol are always afraid that he will come too near the earth and burn it up. Their mythology gives an account of his violent origin. In the distant past, so one legend goes, the earth was inhabited by the animal people, and they longed for the light of a sun. Accordingly they chose a boy and thrust him into the fire. After travelling down through the five levels of the underworld, he emerged with a great eruption as a volcano and rose into the sky, where he became the sun, and each night he is destined to repeat this same journey. The bloody human sacrifice that engendered the sun, so reminiscent of Aztec rituals, shows some of the ambivalence with which this deity is viewed by the Huichol. Christian teachings have done nothing to lessen his importance, and Lumholtz noted down this telling comment by one of his informants: 'If Christians pray to the saints that are made by carpenters, why should not the Huichol pray to the sun which is so much better made?'

Known collectively as 'Our Mothers', the female deities are identified with rain, earth, growth and maize. Chief among them is Nakawé or 'Grandmother Growth', for she was present at the beginning of the world before the others appeared. Her favourite habitation is deep down in the earth, and from her lap come the trees, bushes and plants that provide the Huichol with food. It is to her that requests for a good harvest, long life and the health of children are most often made. The Huichol have their own deluge legend in which 'Grandmother Growth' plays a key role.

One day a Huichol was clearing his fields for planting, when Nakawé appeared and told him that his labour was in vain. She warned him of an approaching flood, and advised him to make a box-shaped boat and to carry with him five grains of maize, five beans, and a black bitch. All this the man did. After five years the waters subsided, and the goddess caused the vegetation and the wildlife to reappear. The man settled down in a cave with his dog, but one afternoon on returning from the fields he was mystified to find tortillas ready for him. At the end of five days, he decided to satisfy his curiosity and find out who was preparing his food, so he remained behind in hiding. When he saw the black bitch take off her skin, he threw it on to the flames of the fire, and from that time on she remained a woman. Together they had a large family, and their descendants re-peopled the earth.

Stories such as these are regarded as fact by the Huichol people, for they have their own mythological view of history which is passed down orally from generation to generation and jealously guarded by the shamans or *mará'akáte*. It is they who keep the legends alive by chanting them on ceremonial occasions, and as they listen the children learn about their heritage. This is the only formal education that most of them receive.

Huichol folklore is by no means static however, because as new things are absorbed from the outside world, myths evolve which explain them from a Huichol perspective. One example deals with Mexican coins and their adoption by the group. To commemorate the founding of Tenochtitlán by the Aztec after their long journey, the Mexican peso bears the image of an eagle perched on a prickly pear cactus. But because the eagle is the sacred bird of the 'Sun Father', the Huichol say it was their god who ordained that the coins should bear this design, in

A shaman presiding over the Feast of the Ripe Fruits—one of the many festivals that punctuate the Huichol year

order to protect and maintain his people.

There is an enormous body of legends, and *mará'akáte* need to have excellent memories. One anthropologist noted that a shaman of his acquaintance was capable of singing what amounted to over 400 manuscript pages of myths. Physical endurance is another requisite, for there are times when *mará'akáte* need to chant for days and nights on end without sleeping, perpetuating the sacred legends of the gods, and accompanying themselves on the violin.

Huichol shamans are more than singer-priests however. As custodians of the group's traditions, they are also responsible for maintaining the integrity of Huichol society, and for

The shaman waving his sacred wand of bird feathers

enforcing its moral values. It is their duty to give advice to those who ask it. To do wrong in their terms is to live out of harmony with the universe. *Mará'akáte* are also healers who treat the sick by blowing smoke, by administering massages and herbal remedies, or by sucking out the evil that is believed to have caused the illness. This evil is thought of as taking the form of a pebble, a grain of corn or even a lizard, which the shamans appear to remove as a cure. Among the Huichol, sickness is attributed not to natural causes but to the ill-will of the gods, and it is assumed that a patient has brought his misfortune upon himself by falling short in his religious obligations. *Mará'akáte* must also be able to guard those in their charge against the black magic of sorcerors—failed shamans, who have put their knowledge and skill at the service of evil.

Birds' feathers, attached to a stick, are important symbols of office. Magical powers are attributed to birds, because it is thought that they can see and hear everything during their flight above the earth, and their wing and tail feathers are greatly prized. While chanting or curing, the shaman waves his *muvieri*, or plumed wand, in the direction of the four cardinal points, thereby acknowledging the corners of the world which are believed to be upheld by four gigantic Brazil trees. In addition he addresses a fifth point (five is a sacred number among the Huichol), the *axis mundi* or central pole that pierces the several layers of the universe.

A shaman's role is very demanding, intellectually, physically and spiritually, and few can hope to fill it. His conduct should be exemplary, for he must command absolute respect, and his life should be one of total dedication, full of voluntary hardship and privation. Whereas most Huichol have only one soul, *mará'akáte* are thought to have five, and from birth this sets them apart from their fellows. It is normal for a shaman to receive a call from the gods as a young boy, most often from 'Grandfather Fire', who was the First Shaman, and to attach himself to one who is fully fledged, acting as his helper and gradually gaining the knowledge he will need.

Shamans expect to support themselves and their families by farming, although they do get small sums of money for curing and also for presiding over ceremonies within the *rancho*. At such times it is not unusual for their repertoire of myths to include one advocating prompt payment! Other paid duties include officiating during burials, because the souls of the dead need guidance on the long journey that awaits them, and performing naming ceremonies for the newly born. Lumholtz was assured during his stay with the Huichol that there were some people without names, all because their parents had been unable to afford the fee. But on the whole payments are low, and most *mará'akáte* remain poorer than those they serve.

In addition to these local ceremonies which are sponsored by individual families, the Huichol year is punctuated by a number of religious festivals corresponding to the wet and dry seasons, and these are often held in the main ceremonial centres. Quiet and virtually deserted throughout most of the year, these centres fill up during the festive period with large groups of Indians from the surrounding area, many of whom have had to walk long distances through the Sierra, laden with food and gifts for the gods. Each centre has its *calihuey* or great temple, usually surrounded by smaller temples dedicated to individual deities. During festivities, which often last for days and nights on end, the *calihuey* becomes a hospitality centre where visitors can eat and sleep.

Highly creative as a people, the Huichol spend a lot of time and energy preparing for these celebrations, making elaborate offerings which will express their faith and at the same time give a concrete form to their desires. Chief among these offerings are votive arrows, for they carry the requests of the maker straight to the gods. Miniature objects tied to the shaft symbolise special demands. Stuck upright in the ground during ceremonies, the arrows are then thought of as 'sacrificed', and supplicants know that their prayers have been heard. Votive bowls are another favourite gift. These are set out on the ground, together with offerings of food and flowers, and it is hoped that when the gods come to use them, they will drink in the prayers of the faithful and grant what has been asked. Bowls are made by coating the inside of half-gourds with beeswax, and forming decorative designs with seeds, maize kernels, minute pebbles and wads of cotton wool which are pressed down into the wax. Glass beads, introduced into the area by the Spaniards, have proved very popular and today many gourds are entirely lined with them. Pictures convey the hopes of the maker—a hunter might shape a deer to show that he needs divine help on his next hunting expedition.

Similar 'visual prayers', both embroidered and woven, adorn the clothes of the Huichol, who see dress as another important

A finely embroidered costume—the motifs are thought to ward off evil

way of expressing their religious beliefs and communicating with the gods. 'A fine Huichol man in costume is what first enabled the "Sun Father" to rise in the sky and shine,' a shaman once told a visiting anthropologist. Even at non-festive times of the year Huichol dress is among the most striking in Mexico, but on ceremonial occasions families are careful to wear their finest and newest clothes.

Long open-sided shirts and square shoulder capes, folded corner to corner, are worn by the men, with the post-Conquest addition of wide trousers. Made from industrially produced calico, these garments are embroidered in cross stitch with a profusion of symbolic motifs which protect the wearer against harm and evil spirits. Numerous shoulder bags play the part of pockets, while woven waist-sashes of wool hold the trousers in

place, serving at the same time as prayers for rain because their long, winding shape makes them easily identifiable as water snakes. Zigzag patterning, suggestive of lightning, and water bottle gourds are the design motifs most commonly associated with rain, whereas the white totó flower that grows during the wet maize-producing season is both a symbol of, and a petition for, this staple crop. Hats, made from plaited palm and decorated with woollen pompons, clusters of feathers, tassels, seed-pods or bead droplets, complete the male costume.

The Huichol woman wears a blouse and skirt, together with the V-shaped garment of pre-Hispanic origin known throughout Mexico as a *quechquemitl*. Today these clothes are often made from printed squares of brightly coloured cotton cloth, but where calico is still used it is embroidered with stylised

designs similar to those which embellish the male costume. In addition, both sexes deck themselves out with colourful necklaces, pendants, armbands, rings and ear-rings of netted beadwork, which incorporate these same symbolic motifs, many of which appear yet again as painted facial decorations during important festivities.

Although the presiding shaman is often more poorly dressed than other men, in keeping with his disregard for material possessions, he is expected to bring great skill to the making and displaying of his ceremonial offerings, for he is acting on behalf of the community at large. Many of these gifts to the gods are set out in the temples, where their keepers will watch over them, but large numbers are laid out in the open air, near the sacred fire which burns during all festivities. Seated on his bamboo chair with the offerings at his feet, the *mará'akáme* salutes the cardinal points with his feathered wand and sings the legends of the gods, phrases of which are repeated by his two assistants.

It is also the shaman's duty to guide his followers through the complicated rituals that characterise the different festivals, and Lumholtz was full of praise for the Huichol: 'The Indians are always formal and correct in their ceremonies. . . . Everything moves with precision, as if they had watches. The scenes were shifting all the time, yet there were no slips. Many take part in the performance, and everyone knows exactly what to do and when to do it, because they have been rehearsing it all their lives.'

But despite the underlying seriousness of purpose, cheerfulness and humour are essential ingredients at most ceremonies. This is consistent with the Huichol view that religion is a part of life, and not an isolated matter to be approached with caution and solemnity. Food and drink are offered to the gods, while the remainder is shared out and enjoyed by those present. Music and dancing are another feature of Huichol festivals. Although some dance-steps are the result of European influence, many are of Indian origin, and this same fusion of styles is apparent in the music. The fiddle and the guitar, both introduced into the area by the Spaniards, are as important to the Huichol today as their own vertical drum and gourd rattles. Completely within the Mexican Indian tradition, however, are the clowns who amuse onlookers with their antics. Bound by a vow to perform during certain ceremonies, they add a comic dimension to the proceedings. Wearing masks and carrying staffs, they parody the non-Indians of the region—who are collectively known as 'neighbours'—while at the same time keeping order.

These masked figures, who combine humour with discipline, are always present during the rain ceremonies which mark the end of the dry season. The steep slopes of the Sierra do not hold water, and only continuous soaking during the wet season can save the crops from the intense heat of the sun. Feasts are accordingly held throughout the region to ensure that the water goddesses will bring the rains from the East, and cover

the earth once again with the spring flowers that they wear for
a costume.

Dependent for their survival on maize, the Huichol hold
another set of ceremonies to honour the various stages of its
growth, each of which has its own special name. As their staple
food, it must be treated with respect at all times, and farmers are
careful when working in their fields to have only wholesome
thoughts lest they offend it and cause it to do badly. People also
try never to step on the grains for fear of crushing out their life-
force. Because food is a gift of the gods, it is against Huichol lore
to eat a new crop without first making a feast and dedicating a
share of the harvest to the givers. Even the various seasonal
ways of preparing maize have to be celebrated, and different
drinks and food such as maize beer, gruel, *tortillas*, cakes and

tamales are offered to the gods before they can once again become part of the Huichol diet.

Most often held at *rancho* level, these feasts include that of the Seed Maize, the Green Maize, the Roasting Ears when maize is offered to 'Father Sun', and the Parched or Toasted Maize. Known as *Rarikira*, the Feast of the Parched Maize is the last one in the cycle. During the festivities, the shaman invokes the help of the female rain deities for the approaching planting season. The shelled maize is toasted, then ritually fed to 'Grandfather Fire' and to the tools which will be used to clear the land. Throughout the night, participants circle the fire in an anti-clockwise direction, while the shaman sings of the beauty of maize. He tells his followers how he can hear her weeping because she has allowed herself to be toasted, and he asks her forgiveness as he chants her sacred legends. Many of these are very sad, causing him and his hearers to weep, both in sympathy with the maize and out of sorrow for the precarious nature of their own dependence upon it.

Once upon a time the Huichol had no maize and they were always hungry. One day a boy, who lived with his widowed mother, heard that there were men living on the other side of the mountains who knew the secret of maize, and he decided to go and find them. On his way through the mountains he met a group of men who offered to accompany him, and they all went on together. Night fell and the boy slept, but when he woke up the next morning he discovered that his companions, who were not men but ants, had eaten his clothes, his hair, and even his eyelashes. Sitting in a tree above him was a white dove, and she promised to help him and asked him to follow her to her house. On arrival she offered him a gourd of maize gruel and five small *tortillas*. To his surprise, although he ate and drank heartily, the food and drink never grew less. The white dove then regained her human form and explained that she was the mother of maize. Introducing him to her five daughters, each one of whom represented a different kind of maize, she asked him to choose a bride. Passing over the yellow, the red, the white and the mottled, the boy asked to marry the purple daughter because she was the most beautiful, and the mother agreed. But first she made him promise that he would never put her to work, but would cherish and protect her always.

When he arrived home with his new bride, his mother was angry and scolded him for bringing home another mouth to feed. 'Do not worry', the maize girl told her. 'Now that I am here,

The Feast of the Ripe Fruits: women and children play an important part, as this is also a celebration
of fertility

there will always be enough food to eat.' From that time on, the boy's fields were thick with maize, and he built an altar where his young bride could sit. But one day, when he was out of the house, his mother was overcome with jealousy at seeing the maize girl sitting on her altar while she herself had to grind the maize. 'I'm tired of your idleness,' she said. 'Today you too shall work.' Weeping, the boy's bride came down from her altar and began to grind, but all that came out was blood because she was grinding herself. When night came the maize girl left the house never to return, and ever after the Huichol have had to work hard to raise their maize in a constant battle with hunger and hardship.

Squash is another staple food, and during the Feast of the Ripe Fruits the faithful thank the gods for the new harvest. This feast, which takes place in the autumn, is one of the most splendid in the Huichol calendar. The first squashes are brought back to the *rancho* with much rejoicing. Some are set out inside the temple, but others are displayed on a mat with a profusion of offerings. These open-air altars, which surpass those from all other festivals, feature a multitude of votive bowls, embroidered bags, flowers and other gifts. These are surrounded by ceremonial arrows and deer antlers which have been 'planted' in the ground, and festooned with strings of white cotton tufts radiating from a central point and symbolising both the wool-like substance that grows from the squash plant and the white fleecy clouds that bring rain and life to the Huichol.

Gods' eye made with strands of brightly-coloured wool

The Feast of the Ripe Fruits is also a celebration of fertility, and the chief participants are women and children who come dressed in their best clothes. Special attention is paid to heads. Faces are painted with sacred symbols, and the children wear beautifully woven head-bands with feathers, flowers and 'gods' eyes' tucked underneath. Known as *tsikuri*, the 'gods' eyes' are made from strands of brightly-dyed wool which are stretched on to a bamboo cross to form a lozenge through which deities can keep an eye on their followers. Worn by children throughout the festivities, they serve as prayers for health and long life.

During the feast the shaman prays to the squashes, which are often stuck with feathers, and sings songs to them as he accompanies himself on the drum. The most sacred object there, it is hewn from the wood of an oak, covered at one end

Women and children with painted faces shaking their gourd rattles to win the favour of the gods

with deerskin, and decorated with yellow flowers. It was invented—as legend has it—long ago to cure children who were sick. While the women sing, the children help the shaman to win the favour of the gods by shaking their gourd rattles, made from the fruits of a local tree and filled with tiny pebbles. At last the gods reply, speaking through the shaman: they accept the offerings. People and squash have both reached a degree of sacredness and can now safely partake of each other. At dawn the children take food round in bowls as a final offering for the gods, and the ripe squash is eaten by everyone.

The cycle of festivities would not be complete, however, without the many rituals and feasts connected with *peyote*—

A shaman sets out strings of white cotton tufts to symbolise the fluffy rain clouds that bring health and life to the Huichol

the hallucinatory cactus that inspires the Huichol throughout their lives. The cult of this small grey-green plant, known to botanists as *Lophorora Williamsii*, has a long history in Mexico. Fray Bernardino de Sahagún, the Spanish chronicler who described so many aspects of Indian culture, included in his writings an account of nomadic tribes in the Northern deserts who valued *peyote* so highly that they would weep over it, and hold ceremonies in its honour. We know from the same source that the Aztec priests also set great store by *peyote*, using it for divination and to assist in cures, and the name by which this cactus is popularly known today actually derives from the Aztec word '*peyotl*'.

The Way of the Ancestors 215

After the Conquest, the Spaniards tried hard to abolish its use wherever possible, believing it to be the instrument of the devil. But the Huichol and a few other Indian groups in remote surroundings remained faithful to it. The Huichol have their own name for it—'hikuli'. All who take it admit that it is tough and extremely bitter, but say they are rewarded by the brilliantly coloured visions, the heightened perception and the sense of euphoria which are induced by the plant's high mescaline content. Among the Huichol, *peyote* is seen as a divine gift which puts them in touch with the gods.

The cactus is itself a god. According to mythology, *peyote* first appeared on earth as a giant deer, causing small plants to spring up wherever he trod. When the Huichol hunters followed him with their bows and arrows, the deer disappeared, and in his place they found a large *peyote* growing. Among the Huichol, *peyote* is still identified with the deer who is also divine. This magical animal is the hero of numerous legends. Capable of many metamorphoses, he is an incarnation not only of *peyote* but also of maize. Together these three forces form a trinity where each is an incarnation of the other. The complex beliefs and rituals that unite *peyote* and the deer with maize seem to reflect the historical background of the Huichol, with the cult of the deer harking back to their distant origins as nomadic hunters, before maize replaced meat as the staple food.

Wírikúta, the land where the sacred cacti grow, lies far outside Huichol territory in the high desert of San Luis Potosí. Once a year, after the celebration of the Ripe Fruits festival in the autumn, small bands of pilgrims leave their homes and families to walk the 300 miles that separate the tribe from Wírikúta. The journey, which is extremely arduous, is preceded and accompanied throughout by purification rites, fasting and other voluntary hardships. The route almost certainly retraces an earlier migration, and the Huichol talk of this pilgrimage as a return to Paradise, to the land of the Ancestors. The quest for *peyote* is akin to a hunting ritual, and the tiny plants are shot through with bows and arrows as if they were fleeing deer. Although some cacti are eaten during the journey, the majority are carried back with great care and reverence to be shared with the community at home.

Peyote can be taken in several ways. Often the cacti are replanted on arrival in the Sierra and chewed fresh throughout the year, or preserved by hanging on long strings to be eaten dry.

A yarn painting showing a stylised representation of the sacred cactus, *peyote*, floating above a maize plant. The shaman on the left performs a ceremony in their honour (*see also colour plate 38*)

As an alternative, *peyote* can also be drunk ground up in water. The visions that follow are divine and should not be told except by the shaman. But although these mystical experiences remain intensely private, the nature of many visions is conveyed by yarn paintings which have evolved as an art form over recent years. These brilliantly-coloured pictures, made by pressing strands of wool on to beeswax-coated boards to form a mosaic, originated with the *nierika* which means 'countenance' or 'image'.

Like decorated gourds, *nierikas* are tangible prayers showing what the Huichol hope to gain from the gods, and traditionally they are made from stone, or reeds interwoven with yarn, as well as small wooden squares. These offerings, intended to mirror the 'face' of the natural forces, have been elaborated and enlarged to meet an ever-growing demand by galleries and collectors. Today they provide many Huichol with a welcome source of income. Inspired by the memory of *peyote* visions, yarn paintings combine vibrant colours with complex symbols to show the myths and ceremonies of the Huichol people.

The chief festival in honour of *peyote* takes place after the return of the pilgrims from the ancestral desert of Wírikúta. With music, songs and dances they retrace their journey in search of the sacred cactus, while the whole community participates. Until recent years, while the Sierra still sheltered many deer, ceremonies included a hunt. A close bond united the hunters and their prey, and when they killed a deer it was understood that he had offered himself to them and would rise again, as surely as spring follows winter, because his spirit was eternal. Now their numbers are sadly reduced, and hunters often fail to snare one as ritual demands. But the introduction of cattle, made long ago by the Spaniards, has provided the Huichol with an alternative, for blood is sacred to the *peyote* festival. Throughout the night the chosen bull stands tethered, while the ceremonies draw to their climax.

The *mará'akáme*, illuminated by the flames of the fire, chants the legends of *peyote*. He sings of its virtues and recounts the epic struggle which took place in the First Times between the *peyote* god and Kieri, the evil god of the *datura* plant. Although Kieri was beaten, he never died. Today he still lives on as the Tree of the Wind, tempting the foolish to taste his leaves and driving them to madness and even suicide with his hallucinations. The *mará'akáme* urges his followers to remain loyal to *peyote*, and through the hours of darkness many eat the bitter green segments or drink the white liquid from gourds. This helps them keep awake and protects them from the chill night air, while putting them in touch with the gods. With sporadic bursts of energy, dancers perform to the music of the fiddle and guitar. One dance involves the loud and rhythmic stamping of feet, as performers hop from one foot to the other on a narrow plank.

With the first weak light of dawn, the Huichol begin to tidy their clothes. Faces are painted with the emblems of deer and *peyote*, and for this a yellow paste is used, made from the root of a plant which grows in Wírikúta. Men and women both take part in the main dance of the early morning, forming a circle and urged on by the shrill and rasping tones of a bull's horn and by the music of the fiddle and guitar. With the sunrise comes the sacrifice of the bull. The chosen leader slices across the jugular vein with a knife, and, as the blood pumps out, it is

Face painting in preparation for the *peyote* rituals (*see also colour plate 6*)

collected in buckets and used to anoint everything from prayer arrows and ceremonial gourds to the treasured possessions of individuals. This is a time of joking and joy, because the gods have been honoured and their goodwill has been ensured.

In the ceremonial centre of San Andrés Cohamiata, these pagan rituals contrast strangely with the symbols of Christianity left behind by visiting Franciscans during the nineteenth century. An old missionary bell is tolled to announce the moment of sacrifice, and as the bull dies at the foot of a rough wooden cross, its blood spills on to an ancient and sacred

The climax of festivities: the slaughtering of a bull

Huichol stone, carved with the image of a coiled serpent.

Despite these seeming contradictions and the absorption by the local Huichol of these alien features, beliefs and ceremonies have altered very little over the years. But San Andrés, which is a relatively outlying community, is at the heart of a new drive by the Mexican government to bring remote Indians into the national orbit. The Instituto Nacional Indigenista is responsible for improving living standards in the area. With this end in view an airstrip has been built nearby, together with a number of tin-roofed centres that include an agricultural station, a carpentry studio, an infirmary and a school. However, San Andrés remains little more than a meeting place. Only a few families live there, and neighbouring Huichol come in only for important events or religious ceremonies, preferring to follow a traditional pattern of life and to keep to the ways of their ancestors. Many Huichol leaders are actually hostile to the idea of schools. In the words of one informant: 'If our sons go to school, they will lose their native tongue and their beliefs. Then they will no longer want to worship the Sun and the Rain.'

It seems as if, for a while longer at least, these Indians of the Western Sierra Madre will continue to serve their gods in their own way. The ancient myths will be passed on to the next generation, who will carry on the ceremonial cycle of rituals and pilgrimages. Future shamans will still lead their followers on the long journey to Wírikúta, the ancestral lands where the *peyote* cactus grows. They too will chant the sacred songs of the Huichol race, like this one in honour of Wírikúta:

> What beautiful hills, what beautiful hills,
> so green here where we are.
> Do not weep, brothers, do not weep,
> we have come here to be happy,
> we have taken this path
> to find our lives.
>
> For we are all,
> we are all the children
> of a flower of brilliant colours,
> of a burning flower.
> And here there is no one
> who regrets what we are.

* * *

Picture Acknowledgements

Picture research by Naomi Narod

Colour Plates (following pages 64 and 128)

1 Rosalind Bentley; 2 Anna Benson Gyles; 3 Chloë Sayer; 4 Marcos Ortiz; 5 Chloë Sayer; 6 Marcos Ortiz; 7 Chloë Sayer; 8 Anna Benson Gyles; 9 Chloë Sayer; 10, 11, 12, 13 Anna Benson Gyles; 14 Werner Forman Archive; 15 GHS Bushnell; 16 Werner Forman Archive; 17 Anna Benson Gyles; 18 Photographie GIRAUDON; 19, 20 Lee Boltin; 22 Werner Forman Archive; 23 *left* Anna Benson Gyles; *right* Rosalind Bentley; 24 Chloë Sayer; 25 Marcos Ortiz; 26 Rosalind Bentley; 27 Museo Nacional de Antropológia; 28 Marcos Ortiz; 29, 30, 31 David Attenborough; 32 Marcos Ortiz; 33 David Bennett; 34 Marcos Ortiz; 35 Anna Benson Gyles; 36 Marcos Ortiz; 37 Anna Benson Gyles; 38 BBC

Black and White

Endpaper maps and chart p8 Line and Line; page 10, 12 Anna Benson Gyles; 15 Chloë Sayer; 17, 19 Ruth Lechuga; 21 Rosalind Bentley; 22 *left and right* BBC; 23 Photographie GIRAUDON; 24, 25, 27 Museo Nacional de Antropológia; 30 Anna Benson Gyles; 31 Ferdinand Anton; 32 Lee Boltin; 33 Ferdinand Anton; 34 BBC; 35 Chloë Sayer; 36 Ferdinand Anton; 37 *top* Museo Nacional de Antropológia; *below* Lee Boltin; 38 *top* Lee Boltin; *below* Kodansha Ltd/Museo Nacional de Antropológia; 39 Lee Boltin; 40 Photo Boudot–Lamotte; 42 Rosalind Bentley; 43 Photo Boudot–Lamotte; 44 *top and below* Ferdinand Anton; 45 *top* Lee Boltin; *below* Ferdinand Anton; 47 Lee Boltin; 48 *top and right* Chloë Sayer; 49 Ruth Lechuga; 51 *top* Anna Benson Gyles; *below* BBC; 52 *top, middle* Lee Boltin; *below* CLaus Hansmann; 53 *top* Werner Forman Archive; *below* Ferdinand Anton; 54 19th-Century engraving by Jose Guadalupe Posada; 55 Ruth Lechuga; 56 David Attenborough; 57 *top and below*, 58, 61, 62, 63 *top and lower* Ferdinand Anton; 64 Anna Benson Gyles; 65 *top* Anna Benson Gyles; *below* BBC; 66 BBC; 67 Anna Benson Gyles; 68 Museo Nacional de Antropológia; 71 BBC; 72 *top* Ferdinand Anton; *below* David Attenborough; 73 BBC; 74 Werner Forman Archive; 75 Photo Boudot–Lamotte; 76 *top* Courtesy Trustees British Museum; *below* BBC; 77 *top* Courtesy Trustees British Museum; *below* Ferdinand Anton; 79 Courtesy Trustees British Museum; 80 Chloë Sayer, 81 Ruth Lechuga; 82 Chloë Sayer; 83 *left* Rosalind Bentley; *right* Werner Forman Archive; 84 Ferdinand Anton; 85 Werner Forman Archive; 87 Rosalind Bentley; 88 Ferdinand Anton; 89 *left* Foto Marburg; *right* Ferdinand Anton; 90 Photographie GIRAUDON; 91 Ferdinand Anton; 92 Roger–Violett/Museo Nacional de Antropológia; 93 Ruth Lechuga; 94 Rosalind Bentley; 97 *left* Rosalind Bentley; *right* Lee Boltin; 98 *left and right* Ferdinand Anton; 99 Lee Boltin; 100, 101 Chloë Sayer; 102, 103 BBC; 104 Ferdinand Anton; 105 *top* Lee Boltin; *below* Roger–Violett; 107, 108 *top and lower* Ferdinand Anton; 109 David Attenborough; 111 Rosalind Bentley; 113, 114 *top and lower* Ruth Lechuga; 115 *top* Ruth Lechuga; *lower* Werner Forman Archive; 117 Ruth Lechuga; 118 Marcos Ortiz; 119 *top* Marcos Ortiz; *below* Rosalind Bentley; 121 David Bennett; 124 Ferdinand Anton; 126 Roger–Violett; 128, 129, 130 Lee Boltin; 131 Courtesy Trustees British Museum; 133 Anna Benson Gyles; 134 Courtesy Trustees British Museum; 135 Ruth Lechuga; 137 Anna Benson Gyles; 138, 139, 141 Ruth Lechuga; 143, 144 Roger–Violett; 145 Courtesy Trustees British Museum; 146 Roger–Violett; 149 Photo Boudot–Lamotte; 150 Anna Benson Gyles; 151 Roger–Violett; 152 Photographie GIRAUDON; 153 Anna Benson Gyles; 154 Roger–Violett; 155, 156 Werner Forman Archive; 158 Photo Boudot–Lamotte; 159 Roger–Violett; 160 Photographie GIRAUDON; 161 Photo Boudot–Lamotte; 162 Lee Boltin; 165 Chloë Sayer; 166 Marcos Ortiz; 167 Stills from 16 mm film BBC; 168 Anna Benson Gyles; 169 Chloë Sayer; 170 Still from 16 mm film BBC; 172, 175, 177, 179, 180, 181, 182, 183 Marcos Ortiz, 184 Anna Benson Gyles; 185, 187 *top and bottom*; 188, 189, 191 Marcos Ortiz; 192 *left* Rosalind Bentley; *right* Marcos Ortiz; 193 Ruth Lechuga; 196, 198, 199 Chloë Sayer; 201, 203, 204 Ruth Lechuga; 206, 207 Chloë Sayer; 208 Anna Benson Gyles; 210 Marcos Ortiz; 212 Ruth Lechuga; 213 Anna Benson Gyles; 214, 215 Ruth Lechuga; 217 BBC; 218 Ruth Lechuga; 219 *top* Chloë Sayer; *below* Marcos Ortiz.

Bibliography

ACOSTA, Jorge R. and other contributors
1970   *Teotihuacán, Lugar de los Dioses*
A collection of essays
(Artes de Mexico, No. 134, Mexico City)

ACOSTA, Padre Joseph de
1880   *The Natural and Moral History of the Indies*
(Hakluyt Society, London)

ADAMSON, David
1975   *The Ruins of Time*
(George Allen and Unwin Ltd., London)

ANALES DE CUAUHTITLAN
1885   *Anales del Museo Nacional de Mexico,*
Tomo 3, Appendix
(Mexico)

ATTENBOROUGH, David
1976   *The Tribal Eye*
(BBC Publications, London)

BARRERA V., Alfredo and other contributors
1969   *Mitos, Ritos y Hechicerias*
essays by various authors
(Artes de Mexico No. 124, Mexico City)

BARRIOS, Virginia B. de
1971   *A Guide to Tequila, Mezcal and Pulque*
(Editorial Minutiae Mexicana, Mexico
City)

BEALS, Ralph L.
1932   *The Comparative Ethnology of Northern
Mexico before 1750*
(Ibero-Americana, 2, University of
California, Berkeley)
1969   *'Southern Mexican Highlands and Adjacent
Coastal Regions: Introduction'* in *Handbook
of Middle American Indians*, Vol. 7, edited
by Evon Z. Vogt.
(University of Texas Press, Austin)

1975   *The Peasant Marketing System of Oaxaca,
Mexico*
(University of California Press)

BENÍTEZ, Ana M. de
1976   *Pre-Hispanic Cooking*
(Bilingual Edition in Spanish and English,
Ediciónes Euroamericanas Klaus Thiele,
Mexico)

BENITÉZ, Fernando
1968   *En la Tierra Magica del Peyote*
(Ediciónes Era, S.A., Mexico)

BERNAL, Ignacio
1970   *The Mexican National Museum of
Anthropology*
(Revised edition, Thames and Hudson,
London)

BLOM, Frans
—— **and DUBY, Gertrude**
1955–7 *La Selva Lacandona* (2 vols)
(Editorial Cultura, Mexico City)

—— **and DUBY, Gertrude**
1969   *'The Lacandón'* in *Handbook of Middle
American Indians*, Vol. 7, edited by Evon
Z. Vogt.
(University of Texas Press, Austin)
1971   *The Conquest of Yucatán*
(Cooper Square Publishers Inc., New
York)

BRAIN, Robert
1972   *Into the Primitive Environment*
(George Philip & Son Ltd., London)

BRAY, Warwick
1968   *Daily Life of the Aztecs*
(G. P. Putnam Sons, New York)

BRUCE S., Roberto D.
1968   *Gramática del Lacandón*
(Depto. de Investigaciones
Antropológicas, I.N.A.H.—Pub. No. 21,
Mexico City)
1971   *Los Lacandónes: 2 Cosmovisión Maya*
(Depto. de Investigaciones

Antropológicas, I.N.A.H.—Pub. No. 27, Mexico City)

1974 *El Libro de Chan K'in*
(No. 12 de la Serie Científica, I.N.A.H. Mexico City)

1975 *Lacandón Dream Symbolism*
Volume 1, Dream Symbolism and Interpretation
(Ediciónes Euroamericanas Klaus Thiele, Mexico)

1976 *Lacandón Texts and Drawings from Najá*
(Trilingual Edition in English, Spanish and Maya: No. 45 de la Serie Científica, I.N.A.H. Mexico City)

BULLOCK, W.

1824 *Six Months' Residence and Travel in Mexico*
(John Murray, London)

BURLAND, Cottie

1975 *Feathered Serpent and Smoking Mirror*
(Orbis Publishing, London)

BUSHNELL, G. H. S.

1967 *Ancient Arts of the Americas*
(Revised Edition, Thames and Hudson, London)

1978 *The First Americans*
(Thames and Hudson, London)

CALI, François

1961 *The Art of the Conquistadors*
(Thames and Hudson, London)

CARMICHAEL, Elizabeth

The British and the Maya
(The British Museum, London)

CASO, Alfonso

1932 'Monte Albán, Richest Archaeological Find in America'
(The *National Geographic Magazine*, Vol. 62, pp. 487–512, Washington)

1958 *The Aztecs, People of the Sun*
(Oklahoma Press, Norman)

—— and GUTIÉRREZ, Tonatiúh

1965 *El Deporte Prehispanico*

(Artes de Mexico, Nos. 75, 76, Mexico City)

CATHERWOOD, Frederick

1844 *Views of Ancient Monuments in Central America, Chiapas and Yucatán*
(London)

CHEETHAM, Nicolas

1974 *New Spain: The Birth of Modern Mexico*
(Victor Gollancz, London)

CHIÑAS, Beverly L.

1973 *The Isthmus Zapotecs: Case Studies in Cultural Anthropology*
(Holt, Rinehart and Winston, U.S.A.)

CODICES (a selection):

CODEX BORBONICUS (Nahua)
A Pre-Columbian Codex Preserved in the Library of the Chamber of Deputies, Paris

CODEX BORGIA (Probably Nahua)
A Pre-Columbian Codex Preserved in the Ethnographical Museum of the Vatican, Rome

CODEX BOTURINI: TIRA DE LA PEREGRINACIÓN (Nahua)
A Pre-Columbian Codex Preserved in the Librería Anticuaria, Mexico City

CODEX DRESDEN (Maya)
A Pre-Columbian Codex Preserved in the Royal Library, Dresden

CODEX FLORENTINO—*see* Sahagún, Fray Bernardino de

CODEX MENDOZA (MENDOCINO) (Nahua)
A Codex Preserved in the Bodleian Library, Oxford

1978 (Facsimile published by Productions Liber S. A., CH-Fribourg)

CODEX ZOUCHE-NUTTALL (Mixtec)
A Pre-Columbian Codex Preserved in the British Museum, London.

1902 (Facsimile published with an introduction

by Zelia Nuttall, by the Peabody Museum of American Archeology and Ethnology, Cambridge. (republished, without the introduction, by Dover Publications, 1975).

COE, Michael D.
1962   *Mexico: Ancient Peoples and Places*
        (Thames and Hudson, London)
1977   *The Maya*
        (Penguin Books, Harmondsworth)

COOK, Scott and DISKIN, Martin (editors)
1976   *Markets in Oaxaca*
        (University of Texas Press, Austin)

CORDRY, Donald and Dorothy
1968   *Mexican Indian Costumes*
        (University of Texas Press, Austin)

CORTÉS, Hernán
1908   *Letters of Cortés*
        (translated and edited by F. A. MacNutt, 2 vols., New York and London) .

COVARRUBIAS, Miguel
1957   *Indian Art of Mexico and Central America*
        (New York)

CRUMRINE, N. Ross
1974   *El Ceremonial de Pascua y la Identidad de los Mayos de Sonora*
        (Instituto Nacional Indigenista, Mexico)
1977   *The Mayo Indians of Sonora: A People who Refuse to Die*
        (The University of Arizona Press, Tucson, Arizona)

CRUMRINE, Lynne Scoggins
1969   'Ceremonial Exchange as a Mechanism in Tribal Integration among the Mayos of Northwest Mexico'
        (Anthropological Papers of the University of Arizona, Number 14, University of Arizona Press, Tucson, Arizona)

DAVIES, Nigel
1973   *The Aztecs*
        (Macmillan, London)

DÍAZ DEL CASTILLO, Bernal
1908–16 *The True History of the Conquest of New Spain*
         (translated by A. P. Maudslay, Hakluyt Society, 5 vols., London)

DUBY, Gertrude, *see* **BLOM, Frans**

DURÁN, Fray Diego
1951   *Historia de las Indias de Nueva Espana*
        (Editorial Nacional, S.A., Mexico)

EMMERICH, André
1963   *Art Before Columbus*
        (Simon and Schuster, New York)

ESPEJEL, Carlos
1975   *Ceramica Popular Mexicana*
        (Editorial Blume, Mexico–Barcelona)
1978   *Mexican Folk Crafts*
        (Editorial Blume, Barcelona)

FONADAN
        Ceremonial de Pascua entre los Indigenas Mayos
        (Produced by a team of researchers for FONADAN, Mexico)

FURST, Peter
1968   'The Parching of the Maize, an Essay on the Survival of Huichol Ritual'
        (Acta Ethnologica et Linguistica No. 14, Wien)

——, **MYERHOFF, Barbara, NAHMAD, Salomón and KLINEBERG, Otto**
1972   *El Peyote y los Huicholes*
        (Sep–Setentas, Mexico City)

——, **NAHMAD, Salomón**
1972   *Mitos y Arte Huicholes*
        (Sep–Setentas, Mexico City)

GAGE, Thomas
1969   *Travels in the New World*
        (University of Oklahoma Press)

GÓMARA, Francisco Lopez de
1826   *Historia de las Conquistas de Hernando Cortés* (2 vols.)

(Imprenta de la Testimentaria de Ontiveros, Mexico City)

GRIFFIN, William B.
1969 *'Culture Change and Shifting Population in Central and Northern Mexico'* (Anthropological Papers of the University of Arizona 13, University of Arizona Press)

GRIMES, Joseph E. and HINTON, Thomas B.
1969 *'The Huichol and Cora'* in *Handbook of Middle American Indians*, Vol. 8, edited by Evon Z. Vogt.
(University of Texas Press, Austin)

GUTIÉRREZ, Tonatiúh and Elektra
1970–71 *El Arte Popular de Mexico* (Artes de Mexico, Mexico City)
1971 *Miccaihuitl, El Culto a la Muerte* A collection of essays by various contributors
(Artes de Mexico, Mexico City)
1976 *Danzas y Bailes Populares* (Editorial Hermes, S.A., Mexico City)

HELFRITZ, Hans
1970 *Mexican Cities of the Gods—An Archaeological Guide* (Praeger Publishers, U.S.A.)

HONOUR, Hugh
1975 *The New Golden Land* (Pantheon Books, New York)

HORCACITAS, Fernando
1979 *The Aztecs Then and Now* (Editorial Minutiae Mexicana, Mexico City)

INNES, Hammond
1969 *The Conquistadors* (Collins, London)

INSTITUTO NACIONAL INDIGENISTA
1977 *Los Lacandones, Los Mayas, Los Tzeltales, Nahaus de la Sierra Madre Oriental, Los Totonacas* and *Los Huicholes* (Pamphlets published in Mexico City)

JOHNSON, William Weber
1961 *Mexico* (Life World Library Series, Time-Life International)

KAMPEN, Michael Edwin
1972 *The Sculptures of El Tajín, Veracruz* (University of Florida Press, Gainesville)

KELLY, Isabel and PALERM, Angel
1952 *The Tajín Totonac* US Government Printing Office, Washington DC)

—— and HARVEY, H. R.
1969 *'The Totonac'* in *Handbook of Middle American Indians*, Vol. 8, edited by Evon Z. Vogt.
(University of Texas Press, Austin)

LANDA, Fr. Diego de
1941 *Relación de las Cosas de Yucatán* Translated and Edited, with notes by Alfred M. Tozzer
(Papers of the Peabody Museum of American Archeology and Ethnology, Harvard University, Cambridge, Massachusetts, USA)

LAS CASAS, Bartolomé de
1909 *Apologética Historia de las Indias* Nueva Biblioteca de Autores Españoles, Historiadores de Indias Vol. 1 Madrid

LEANDER, Birgitta
1972 *Herencia Cultural del Mundo Náhuatl* (Sep-Setentas, Mexico)

LEÓN PORTILLA, Miguel
1959 *Vision de los Vencidos* (Ediciones de la Universidad Nacional de Mexico)
1963 *Aztec Thought and Culture* Translated by Jack Emory Davis (University of Oklahoma Press, Norman)
1967 *Trece Poetas de Mundo Azteca* (Instituto de Investigaciones Históricas, Universidad Nacional Autónoma de Mexico)

1973   *Los Antiguos Mexicanos*
        (Fondo de Cultura Economica, Mexico
        City)

LUMHOLTZ, Carl
1900   *Symbolism of the Huichol Indians*
        (American Museum of Natural History,
        Mem. Anthr. vol. 2, No. 1)
1903   *Unknown Mexico*, 2 vols.
        (Macmillan, London)

McQUOWN, Norman A.
1956   *The Classification of the Maya Languages*
        (Intl. J. American Linguistics, Vol. 22)

MADSEN, William
1969   'The Nahua' in *Handbook of Middle
        American Indians*, Vol. 8, edited by Evon
        Z. Vogt.
        (University of Texas Press, Austin)

        —— and CLAUDIA
1969   *A Guide to Mexican Witchcraft*
        (Editorial Minutiae Mexicana, Mexico
        City)

MANRIQUE, C. Leonardo
1969   'The Otomi' in *Handbook of Middle
        American Indians*, Vol. 8, edited by Evon
        Z. Vogt.
        1University of Texas Pres, Austin)

MATA TORRES, Ramón
1960   *Vida y Arte de los Huicholes*
        (2 Vols. Artes de Mexico, Nos. 160, 161,
        Mexico City)

MEDINA, Andrés and QUEZADA, Noemí
1975   *Panorama de las Artesanías Otomíes del
        Valle del Mezquital*
        (Universidad Autónoma de México,
        Instituto de Investigaciones
        Antropológicas)

MODIANO, Nancy
1973   *Indian Education in the Chiapas Highlands:
        Case Studies in Cultural Anthropology*
        (Holt, Rinehart and Winston, New York).

MORLEY, Sylvanus G.
1946   *The Ancient Maya*
        (Revised by George W. Brainerd, Stanford
        University Press, Stanford, California)

MULLER, Florence and HOPKINS, Barbara
1974   *A Guide to Mexican Ceramics*
        (Editorial Minutiae Mexicana, Mexico
        City)

MYERHOFF, Barbara G
1974   *Peyote Hunt: The Sacred Journey of the
        Huichol Indians*
        (Cornell University Press, New York)

NADER, Laura
1969   'The Zapotec of Oaxaca' in *Handbook of
        Middle American Indians*, Vol.7, edited by
        Evon Z. Vogt.
        (University of Texas Press, Austin)

NELSON, Ralph
1977   *The Popol Vuh, The Sacred Book of the
        Ancient Quiché-Maya*
        Translated from the Maya by Ralph
        Nelson
        (Houghton Mifflin, Boston)

PARSONS, Elsie C.
1936   *Mitla: Town of the Souls*
        (University of Chicago Press, Chicago)

PAZ, Octavio
1967   *The Labyrinth of Solitude: a Dramatic
        Portrait of the Mexican Mind*
        (Translated by Lysander Kemp, Allen
        Lane, the Penguin Press, London)

PRESCOTT, William H.
1922   *The Conquest of Mexico*
        (Edited by T. A. Joyce and illustrated by
        Keith Henderson, 2 vols, New York)

PRICE, Christine
1972   *Heirs of the Ancient Maya*
        (Charles Schribner's Sons, New York)

PROSKOURIAKOFF, Tatiana
        Historial Implications of a Pattern of Dates

at *Piedras Negras, Guatemala*
(American Antiquity, Vol. 25, Salt Lake City)

RAGGHIANTI, Carlo Ludovico and RAGGHIANTI, Licia
1971 *National Museum of Anthropology, Mexico City: Great Museums of the World*
(The Paul Hamlyn Publishing Group Ltd., Middlesex)

RAMIREZ V., Pedro
1968 *The National Museum of Anthropology*
(Harry N. Abrahams, Inc., New York)

RAVICZ, Robert and ROMNEY, A. Kimbell
1969 '*The Mixtec*' in *Handbook of Middle American Indians*, Vol. 7, Edited by Evon Z. Vogt.
(University of Texas Press, Austin)

ROYS, Ralph L.
1967 *The Book of Chilam Balam of Chumayel*
Translated from the Maya by Ralph L. Roys with notes.
(University of Oklahoma Press, Norman)

RUBÍN DE LA BORBOLLA, Daniel F.
1951 *Native Dress of the Sierra de Puebla*
(Museo Nacional de Artes e Industrias Populares, Mexico City)
1963 *Arte Popular Mexicano*
(Artes de Mexico, Instituto Nacional Indigenista, Mexico City)

RUZ LHUILLIER, Alberto
1952 *Palenque, fuente inagotable de tesoros arqueológicos*
(Mexico de Hoy, Vol IV, No. 48)
1953 *Suntuoso sepulcro en la cripta de Palenque*
(Mexico de Hoy, Vol V, No. 55)
1963 *La Civilización de los antiguos Mayas*
(*Instituto Nacional de Antropológia e Historia, Mexico City*)

SAHAGÚN, Fray Bernardino de
1950– *Florentine Codex: General History of the Things of New Spain*

Editors and Translators from the Náhuatl Language: Charles E. Dibble and Arthur J. O. Anderson
(U.S.A.: Santa Fé School of American Research and University of Utah, Salt Lake City)

SAYER, Chloë
1977 *Crafts of Mexico*
(Aldus Books, London)

SEJOURNÉ, Laurette
1959 *Un Palacio en la Ciudad de los Dioses: Exploraciones en Teotihuacán, 1955–56*
(Instituto Nacional de Antropológia e Historia, Mexico City)

SODI. M., Demetrio
1976 *The Maya World*
(Editorial Minutiae Mexicana, Mexico City)

SOUSTELLE, Jacques
1961 *Daily Life of the Aztecs*
(translated by Patrick O'Brian, Weidenfeld and Nicolson, London)
1971 (translated by E. Ross, André Deutsch, London)

SMITH, Bradley
1975 *Mexico: A History in Art*
(Phaidon Press, London)

SPICER, Edward H.
1969 '*Northwest Mexico: Introduction*' and '*The Yaqui and the Mayo*' in *Handbook of Middle American Indians*, Vol. 8, edited by Evon Z. Vogt
(University of Texas Press, Austin)

STEN, María
1974 *The Mexican Codices and their Extraordinary History*
(English Edition: Ediciones Lara, Mexico City)
1974 *Vida y Muerte del Teatro Náhuatl*
(Sep-Setentas, Mexico City)

STEPHEN, John Lloyd

1841   *Incidents of Travel in Central America, Chiapas and Yucatán* (2 vols) (New York)

1843   *Incidents of Travel in Yucatán* (2 vols) (New York)

THOMPSON, J. Eric

1954   *The Rise and Fall of Maya Civilization* (University of Oklahoma Press, Norman, Oklahoma)

1955   *Bonampak* (Publication No. 602, Carnegie Institute)

1958   *Civilization of the Mayas* (Hatchards, London)

1960   *Maya Hieroglyphic Writing — An Introduction* Second Edition (University of Oklahoma Press, Norman, Oklahoma)

1963   *Maya Archeologist* (University of Oklahoma Press, Norman, Oklahoma)

1970   *Maya History and Religion* (University of Oklahoma Press, Norman, Oklahoma)

1972   *Maya Hieroglyphs without Tears* (British Museum, London)

TOOR, Frances

1947   *A Treasury of Mexican Folkways* (Mexico Press, Mexico City)

TORQUEMADA, Juan de

1943   *Los Veinte y un Libros Rituales: Monarquía Indiana* (3 vols) (Mexico)

TOZZER, Alfred M.

1907   *A Comparative Study of the Mayas and the Lacandones* (Macmillan, London)

VAILLANT, George C.

1965   *The Aztecs of Mexico* (revised by Susannah B. Vaillant, Penguin Books, Harmondsworth and New York)

VASCONCELOS, José

1944   *Breve Historia de Mexico*
(Porrua Hnos., Mexico City)

VILLA ROJAS, Alfonso

1969   'The Tzeltal' in *Handbook of Middle American Indians*, Vol. 7, edited by Evon Z. Vogt (University of Texas Press, Austin)

VOGT, Evon Z.

1969   'The Maya: Introduction' and 'Chiapas Highlands' in *Handbook of Middle American Indians*, Vol. 7. Editor of Vol. 7 and Vol. 8 (University of Texas Press, Austin)

VON HAGEN, Victor Wolfgang

1973   *The Ancient Sun Kingdoms of the Americas* (Paladin, London)

WAUCHOPE, Robert

1964—   General Editor of the *Handbook of Middle American Indians*, (University of Texas Press, Austin)

WILLEY, Gordon R.

1966   *An Introduction to American Archeology* Vol. I: North and Middle America (Prentice Hall, Eaglewood Cliffs, New Jersey)

WOLF, Eric R.

1959   *Sons of the Shaking Earth* (University of Chicago Press, Chicago)

ZINGG, Robert Morley

1938   *The Huichols: Primitive Artists* (G. E. Stechert & Co., New York)

Index

Archaeological sites and major Indian cultures have been given blanket listings. If readers wish to follow up certain aspects, as for example crafts, sculpture or writing systems, then these must be looked up under the theme headings. Illustrations are indexed in brackets after text references; italic figures refer to page numbers of black and white illustrations, bold figures to colour plates (see note on Contents).

Abbreviations: Pre-C (Pre-Conquest) and Post-C (Post-Conquest), Codex ill. (Codex illustration).

Acapulco, 114
Agave, see Maguey
Agriculture, Pre-C, 30, 87; Aztec, 71, 72; Maya, 123, 127, 148; Zapotec, 97; Post-C, 9, 10, 16, 20; Huichol, 195, 197, 204; Lacandón, 137, 138, 140, 148; Maya, 164, 168; Mayo, 174, 181, 182; Mixtec, 112; Nahua, 80 (10, 30); Otomí, 63, 64; Totonac, 48 (48); Zapotec, 92, 95, 96
Agricultural rites, 20, 33, 44, 48, 49, 50, 80, 81, 82, 109, 116, 167, 209, 210, 211, 213, 214
All Souls' Day, see Day of the Dead
Altars, Pre-C, 53; Olmec, 30 (31); Maya, 164; Temple of the Warriors (Chichén Itzá), 160; Totonac, 52; Tula, 61; Xochicalco, 57; Post-C: Huichol, 213 (212); Day of the Dead (27); Totonac altar for the Dead, 54 (55)
Amatenango del Valle, 165–6
Americas, migration to, 29
Animals, see Game, Livestock and Sacrifice
Annals of Cuauhtitlan, 59–60
Architecture, see Ballcourts, Burials, Corbel Arch, Lintels, Mounds, Observatories, Palaces, Pyramids, Sculpture, Temples, Wall paintings. See also site listings
Arithmetic, see Numerical systems
Armengol, Andrés and Juan, 109–10
Asia, 29
Astrology, 22, 76, 77, 128, 164
Astronomy, 23, 57, 58, 81, 90, 91, 120, 128, 129, 132, 137, 140, 148, 164
Atlantic Ocean, 87
Atoyac River, 91
Augustinians, 12
Aztec civilisation, 12, 18, 23, 39, 59, 63, 65–79, 80, 83–6, 88, 111, 151, 163, 195, 201, 202, 215 (23, 27, 34, 66–85)
Aztlán, 65

Bacavachi, 174–94
Baja California, 173
Ball courts, 50–2; Chichén Itzá, 160 (160); Copán, 129, 131; El Tajín, 50, 52 (51, 53); Monte Albán, 91; Xochicalco, 57 (58)
Ball game, 50–3, 160 (Codex ill. 51)
Bark cloth, 142, 167; drink, 167; paper, 164
Bas reliefs, see Sculpture
Basketry, 16, 114, 124
Bat God, 91, 98 (91)
Battles, see Warfare
Beans, 10, 15, 16, 48, 73, 95, 112, 117, 140, 174, 198, 202
Belize, 9, 120, 123, 124
Bible, 18, 177, 178, 182, 184
Bonampak, 142–5 (143, 144)
Brides of Christ, 187, 188 (188)
British invasion, 14
Burials, Pre-C: Maya: Kaminaljuyú, 125; Palenque, 149–51 (151); Tikal, 125; Monte

Albán: early, 91; Mixtec, 105–6, 109 (107, 108), see also Gold, Mixtec; Zapotec, 91, 97–8, 102 (98); Tlatilco, 36–8 (36)
Post-C: Clay burial scenes, 54; Huichol, 204, 205; Mixtec, 116
Burial urns, 97–9 (97–9)

Cacaxla, 21 (21; 23)
Calendar stone, 23 (77)
Calendar systems, 11, 31, 46, 50, 58, 59, 77, 90, 103, 120, 125, 127–9, 132
Campeche, 11, 120
Cardenas, Lazaro, 11
Cardinal points, 18, 49, 81, 190, 204, 209
Caribbean Sea, 9
Carvings, see Sculpture
Casa del Museo, see Museum, mobile
Caso, Alfonso, 105, 106, 109
Catherwood, Frederick, 145, 164
Ceiba tree, 167–8
Celts, Olmec, 33 (20)
Cenote (sacred well), 161 (161)
Ceremonies, Pre-C, 18, 22, 44, 49, 50, 53, 64; Aztec, 73, 76; Maya, 123, 132, 148, 149, 164; Xipe Totec rituals, 109; Post-C, 18–20; Huichol, 195, 202–5, 209–20 (203–19; 6, 37); Jaguar Dance, 33–6 (35; 24–8); Lacandón, 137, 142, 166–70 (167, 170); Maya, 166; Mayo, 171, 176–94 (172, 177–93); 35, 36); Mixtec, 116; Nahua, 80–2 (82; 33); Totonac, 48–50, 54 (19, 49, 55; 29, 30); Zapotec, 95, 117–19 (118, 119; 34). See also Agricultural rites, Ball game, Dances, Day of the Dead, Sacrifice
Chac, 124, 155–7 (155)
Chacmool figures, 61, 160 (61, 159)
Chalchiuhtlicue, 39
Chan K'in, see Max
Chapalanga River, 198
Chiapas, 11, 12, 87, 120, 123, 124, 131–51, 164–70
Chichén Itzá, 52, 53, 157–62 (158–62; 12, 13)
Chilam Balam, 129, 162–4
Chili Peppers, 10, 16, 92, 112, 117, 140, 198
Chinampas (floating gardens), 66 (67)
Chinantec Indians, 88
Christ, Jesus, 18, 34, 95, 173, 177, 186; Mayo Easter Passion: church image, 186, 194 (187); role taken by performer, 179, 183, 184, 186 (183). See also Brides of Christ
Christianity (Roman Catholicism), 11–13, 17–20, 33, 34, 48–50, 53, 80, 81, 117, 136, 137, 164, 166, 171, 173, 176–8, 182, 186, 187, 190, 195, 199, 201, 219. See also Easter Passion, Missionaries, Priests
Cities, see Guatemala City, Mexico City and site listings
Ciudadela (Teotihuacán), 43
Civil war, 13
Coatlicue, 73, 83 (74)
Cocijo, 97 (97)
Codices, 21, 22 (50, 51, 73, 79); Aztec, 70, 77 (34, 65, 66, 71, 76); Maya, 164; Mixtec, 102–4, 110 (22, 102, 103). See also Sahagún
Colonial period, 12, 13, 15–19, 22, 63, 80, 136, 137, 164, 171, 172, 195, 216
Colossal heads (Olmec), 30, 32 (32)
Conch shell trumpets, 44, 45, 166
Conquest, see Spanish Conquest
Cooking, Post-C 16; Huichol, 210, 211 (199); Lacandón, 140, 166; Mayo, 174, 175, 181, 193 (175, 181); Totonac, 47, 48; Zapotec, 95 (94)
Copal resin (incense), 53, 116, 167, 170 (170)
Copán, 129, 130 (128, 131)
Corbel Arch, 147–9, 154 (10)
Corn, see Maize

Cortés, Hernán, 11, 67, 76, 78. See Feather Dance
Costume, Pre-C: Aztec, 68–73, 83; Ballgame players, 52; Dancers, 33; Ixtle clothing, 64; Maya, 125, 143, 157; Mixtec, 103; Teotihuacán, 45; Tlatilco figurines, 36–7; Tula warriors, 61. For photos see Codices, Sculpture etc.
Post-C: 16; Huichol, 205–8, 213; Jaguar Dance, 34; Lacandón, 136, 142; Maya, 164; Mayo, 175; Easter Passion costumes, 181–2, 184, 187–8, 191; Mixtec, 114–16; Nahua, 81; Otomí, 64; Quetzal Dance, 81; Totonac, 48; Tzeltal Maya, 165; Zapotec Feather Dance 118–19. For photos see Indian groups, Dances etc.
Coyolxauhqui, goddess and ceremonial stone, 83 (83)
Crafts, Pre-C: Maya, 123, 124; Mixtec, 23; Zapotec, 23.
Post-C: 10, 16–17, 20; Huichol, 205, 209, 213, 217, 218 (201); Maya, 164; Mayo, 175; Mixtec, 113–14. See also Basketry, Fondo para el Fomento de las Artesanias, Metalworking, Nierika, Potting, Weaving, Woodcarving
Creoles, 13
Cross, its indigenous significance, 18, 49, 148, 190; Huichol missionary cross, 219; Mayo, 173–90; Temple of the Cross (Palenque), 148; Temple of the Foliated Cross (Palenque), 148, (10)
Cruz, Celestino, 95–6, 117–19
Cuauhtemoc, 78–9
Cuetzalan, 81–2
Cuicatec Indians, 88
Cuicuilco, 38–9, 127 (38)
Cuitlahuac, 78
Culhuacan, 59

Dancer slabs, 89–91 (89)
Dances, 18, 19, 37, 70, 81, 143, 161; Deer Dance, 193 (193); Feather Dance, 117–19 (118, 119; 34); God of the Dance (Macuilxochitl), 117–18; Huichol dances, 209, 218; Jaguar (or Tiger) Dance, 33–6 (35; 24–8); Paskola Dance, 180, 190–4 (191, 192); Quetzal Dance, 81–2 (82; 33); Voladores (or Flyers') Dance, 49–50 (49, 50; 29, 30)
Date inscriptions, 31–2, 58–9, 90, 109, 124–5, 127–9, 132–3, 142, 147, 151, 153. See also Stelae
Datura, 218
Day of the Dead, Post-C, 53–4 (27; 31); Totonac 54 (55); Pre-C, celebrations, 53, 64
Death, Avenue of the Dead (Teotihuacán), 42; Cult of Death (Pre-C), 54–5; Flowers of Death, 53–4; Notions about Death, Pre-C: Aztec, 84–6; Post-C: 53–4; Huichol, 204–5; Mixtec, 116; Representations of Death, 37, 54, 95 (37, 54). See also Burials, Day of the Dead, Gods of Death and Bat God, Sacrifice
Deer, 68, 112; Carved bones, 106; Deer Dance, 193 (193); Huichol associations, 205, 213, 216, 218; Jaguar Dance, 35; Mayo and deer, 182
Deerskin, belts, 52; codices, 21, 103, 164; drum, 214
Díaz, Porfirio, 14
Díaz del Castillo, Bernal, 67–8, 76, 78
Digging sticks, 16, 80, 112, 148, 198 (10)
Dominicans, 12
Dress, see Costume
Drums, 34, 50, 70, 81, 186, 191, 192, 209, 213, 214 (192, 203)
Durango, 195

Dyes, 114

Eagle, 72; Aztec myth, 66; Carved, 63, 160 (63); Huichol design motif (206); myth 202
Eagle Knights: Aztec, 72–3, 84 (72, 76); Maya, 157
Earthquakes, 9
Easter Passion (enacted by Mayo Indians), 171, 177–94 (177–93; 35, 36)
Ecce Homo, 34
Education, 15, 20, 26, 70, 72, 96, 112, 116, 175, 176, 202, 220
Eight Deer, 103–4
El Baúl, 124–5 (125)
El Salvador, 120
El Tajín, 46, 49, 50, 52, 55, 120 (47, 51, 53; 14, 29)

Face painting, 208, 213, 218 (218; 6)
Farming, see Agriculture
Feast of the Ripe Fruits, 213–14 (203, 212–15)
Feather Dance, 117–19 (118, 119; 34)
Feathered Serpent, see Kukulcan and Quetzalcoatl
Feathers, 44, 68, 69, 72, 73, 81, 83, 86, 103, 106, 118, 143, 156, 204, 213; Feathered wand (muvieri), 204 (203, 204)
Festivals, see Ceremonies
Figurines, Pre-C; Maya, 123, 164–5 (115, 130); Mixtec, Olmec, 33 (33; 20, 22); Teotihuacán, 54; Tlatilco, 36–8 (37)
Post-C: Lacandón, 141; Modern inspired by Death, 54
Fire, Gods of, Huehueteotl, 38, 39 (38); Huichol Grandfather Fire, 200, 201, 204, 211; Lacandón God K'ak, 167
Fishing, 16, 112, 140, 174, 198
Flint, knives, 76; points, 29
Flute, 34, 50, 70, 81, 191, 182 (192)
Flyers' Dance, see Voladores
Fondo Nacional para el Fomento de las Artesanias (FONART), 96
Franciscans, 12, 199, 219
Fraternity of the Cult of the Mountains, 180, 190–4. See Deer Dance and Paskola Dance
French invasion, 14
Frescoes, see Wall Painting
Friezes, see Sculpture
Fuerte River Valley, 171

Galan, Juan and Reina, 99–102 (100, 101)
Game animals, 29, 30, 112, 140, 168, 174, 198, 218
General History of the Things of New Spain, see Sahagún
Gods, Pre-C: 18, 39, 55, 73, 90, 97, 117, 127, 129, 133–4, 148, 154; Bat God, 91, 98 (91); Chac (Rain God), 124, 155–7 (155); Chalchiuhtlicue (Goddess of Water), 39; Coatlicue (Goddess of Earth, Life and Death), 73, 83 (74); Cocijo (Rain God), 97 (97); Coyolxauhqui (Moon Goddess), 83 (83); Day Gods, 148; Goddess of Death (Maya), 52–3; Jaguar Cult, 33, 36, 124; Huehueteotl, 38–9 (38); Huitzilopochtli (War God), 55, 65, 66, 69, 78, 83 (65); Kukulcan (Maya Plumed Serpent), 61, 157; Macuilxochitl (God of Dance, Music and Song), 117–18; Maize Gods: Maya, 148, Teotihuacán, 43, Zapotec, 98, 117; Mictlantecuhtli (God of Death): Mixtec, 109 (108), Totonac, 52 (53); Quetzalcoatl (Plumed Serpent), 39, 42, 43, 59–61, 63, 64, 69, 77, 78 (75); Sun Gods: Maya, 148, Zapotec, 117; Tezcatlipoca ('The Smoking Mirror', War God), 55, 59–61, 63, 65, 69, 77; Tlaloc (Rain God), 39, 42–4, 69, 83; Tonantzin (Earth Goddess), 18; Xipe

Totec (The Flayed One, God of Spring), 97–8, 109 (77, 98; 18); Xochipilli (God of Music, Song and Love), (23)
Post-C: Gods as natural forces, 20; Huichol, 200–20; See Deer, Fire, Maize, Peyote, Rain, Sun; Lacandón, 133, 134, 137, 166–70; Kisin (God of Death), 167. See Hachakyum, Rain, Sun, Mayo, links old gods and Christianity, 176; Totonac, 48–9
Gods' eyes, 213 (213)
Gold, 11, 13, 60, 68–70, 86, 105; Maya goldware, 161; Mixtec goldware, 105–6 (108; 18, 19)
Goldsmiths' patron god, Xipe Totec, 97, 98, 109 (77, 78; 18)
Goldworking techniques, Pre-C, 109 (Codex ill. 109); Post-C, 110
Gomara, Lopez de, 33
Gomez, Benacio, 178, 184, 187–90 (179)
Grinding stones, 48, 123
Guatemala, 120–5, 129, 131, 151
Guatemala City, 120
Guerrero, 34–6, 87, 111
Guitar, 209, 218
Gulf Coast of Mexico, 9, 23, 45, 60, 73; Huastec area, 123; Olmec area, 30–3, 36, 89, 124; Totonac area, 46–50, 52, 54

Hachakyum, 166–70; Hachakyum's Temple (134, 170)
Hachas, 52 (52)
Hammond, Norman, 123
Handicrafts, see Crafts
Harp, 191
Henequen, 68
Hidalgo y Costillo, Father Miguel, 13
Hieroglyphs, 21, 31–2, 45, 57–9, 89–91, 109, 124, 125, 127, 129, 132, 137, 147, 151, 153, 164, (128, 129). See also Date inscriptions; Numerical and Writing systems
Honduras, 120, 129, 131
Housing, Pre-C; Maya, 148, 156 (156); Monte Albán, 91; Teotihuacán, 42, 43 Post-C, 15, 16, 20, 27; Huichol, 197 (198); Lacandón, 137, 140; Mayo, 174, 175; Mixtec, 112–13 (171, 173); Otomí, 63; Totonac, 47–8; Zapotec, 94–5, 99
Huastec Indians, 122, 124
Huehueteotl, 38, 39 (38)
Huichol Indians, 171, 195–220 (196–219; 5, 6, 37)
Huitzilopochtli, 55, 65, 66, 69, 78, 83 (65)
Human sacrifice, see Sacrifice
Hunting, Pre-C and early hunting period, 29, 65, 113, 120, 123, 182, 195, 216; Post-C, 16, 112, 137, 140, 168, 174, 198, 205, 216, 218; Mayo rites akin to hunting ceremony, 184. See also Jaguar Dance

Ice Age, 29
Incense, see Copal resin
Independence of 1821, 13
Indian, see individual listings of groups, languages, etc.
Industry, 10, 11, 14
Instituto Nacional Indigenista (INI), 20, 220
Itzá, 162–3
Itzcoatl, 66
Ixtle (maguey fibre), 64 (64)
Izapa, 124, 125, 127 (124)

Jade, 33, 86, 91, 106, 120, 125, 151, 160, 161
Jaguar, 37, 60, 68; Carved bones, 106 (108); Jaguar cult, 33, 36, 124; Jaguar (or Tiger) Dance, 33–6 (35; 24–8); Jaguar Dynasty,

133; Links with sun, 33, 148; Representations of, 30, 33, 44, 61, 95, 106, 157–60 (44, 133); Song of the Jaguar, 168; Temple of the Jaguar (Chichén Itzá), 160
Jaguar Knights: Aztec, 72, 73, 84 (34, 72); Maya, 143, 157; Maya, 109
Jaina figurines, 164–5 (115, 130)
Jalisco, 195–220
Jesuits, 12, 171, 176, 178, 195
Jesus, see Christ
Jewellery, Pre-C, 72, 106, 109 (109; 19); Post-C, 23, 110, 208
Juárez, Benito, 13–14

Kaminaljuyú, 125, 127
K'in Bor, 140–1, 170
Kings or Angels (Mayo Easter Passion), 187, 188
Kukulcan, 61, 157; Temple-pyramid of Kukulcan (Chichén Itzá), 157. See Quetzalcoatl

Lacandón Indians, 133–42, 148, 166–70, 171 (135–41, 167–70; 2, 3)
Lacanjá, 142
Lake Texcoco, 66
Landa, Bishop Diego de, 151, 153, 161, 164
Languages: Indian, 9, 15, 16, 171; Huichol, 195, 200; Lacandón, 134, 136; Maya, 122, 123, 134, 136, 162, 164; Mayo, 176, 184; Mixtec, 88, 116; Nahuatl (spoken by Aztec, Nahua and Toltec), 23, 65, 73, 79, 80, 111, 215; Oaxacan groups, 88; Otomí, 63; Totonac, 46, 47; Zapotec, 88, 92, 94, 96; Indian language records 22, see also Chilam Balam, Popol Vuh and Sahagún. Non-Indian languages: Latin, 187; Spanish, 16, 20, 92, 94, 116, 184, 187
Las Casas, Bartolomé de, 12
Las Charcas, 123–4
La Venta, 32–3, 124
Lintels, 132–3 (133; 21)
Livestock, 10, 81, 94, 99, 112, 114, 117, 167, 197, 198, 218, 219. See also Poultry
Long Count, 58, 128, 142, 153
Looms, semi-vertical, 175; waist-strap, 16, 45, 114, 164, 165 (114, 115). See also Weaving
Lumholtz, Carl, 196, 199, 201, 209

Macuilzochitl, 117, 118
Maguey cactus, 45, 63, 64 (65)
Maize, 10, 16, 18, 30, 48, 60, 73, 80, 87, 95, 112, 123, 140, 168, 174, 198, 210, 211; Huichol, Maize ceremonies, gods and mythology, 202, 204, 207, 210–13, 216; Lacandón mythology, 166; Maya, Maize God, 148; Mythology, 122
Malinalco, 84
Mammoths, 29, 41
Markets, Pre-C: Aztec (Tenochtitlán), 67–8; Maya, 132 Post-C: 17, 48, 99 (93, 117); Zapotec market at Tlacolula, 92–4 (1)
Masks, 33, 34, 37, 44, 91, 95, 109, 148, 181, 182, 191, 192, 209 (37, 44, 77, 91, 97, 185, 189, 192; 18); Chac masks on façades, 155 (155); Masks of gods, see Burial Urns.
Mathematics, see Numerical systems
Matting, 94, 113, 114, 124, 198
Max, Chan K'in (Old), 137–40, 167, 168, 170 (137, 138, 167)
Max, Chan K'in (Young), 137, 167, 168, 170
Max, K'ayom, 167 (168)
Maximilian, Archduke, 14
Maxtlatzin, 66
Maya; Pre-C: Early Maya, 120–7 (124, 125); Classic Maya, 12, 18, 23, 36, 52, 53, 56, 57,

59, 61, 88, 120, 127–33, 142–64, 171 (*115*, *126–34*, *143–62*; **9–13**, **21**); Quiché Maya, 120, 122; Yucatec Maya, 123, 136, 151, 154, 157, 161
　Post-C: Lacandón, 134–42, 148, 166–70, 171 (*135–41*, *167–70*; **2**, **3**); Maya groups, 164–6; Tzeltal, 165–6, 168 (*165*)
Mayapán, 163
Mayo Indians, 171–94, 195 (*172–93*; **35**, **36**)
Mayo River Valley, 171, 174
Medicine (unorthodox), 19, 94, 167, 204, 215
Mestizos, 13, 114
Metal-working (technology), 39; gold and silver, 105, 106, 109, 110; tin, 110
Metzabok Lake and Community, 137; God of Rain, 167
Mexico City, 9, 10, 14, 21, 23–8 (Mobile museum on outskirts), 36, 61, 83, 84, 96, 118
Mezquital Valley, 63
Mictlantecuhtli, 52, 109 (*53*, *108*)
Mines, 13, 173
Missionaries, during Colonial era, 11, 12, 17, 18, 22, 33, 110, 126, 171, 219; *see* Jesuits. Post-C: Franciscans, 199; Protestants, 20, 136–7
Mitla, 104, 111 (*12*, *104*, *105*)
Mixcoatl, 59
Mixe Indians, 88
Mixtec: *Pre-C*: 23, 88, 102–9, 110–11 (*22*, *102–8*; **18**, **19**)
　Post-C: 88, 111–17 (*114*, *115*, *117*)
Mixteca region (Mixtecapan), 111–17 (*117*)
Moctezuma, *see* Montezuma
Monte Albán, 120 (*88–92*; **15**); Early phase, 89–91; Mixtec phase, 105, 106, 109; Zapotec phase, 91, 92, 96, 97
Montezuma, 69, 70, 76, 78. *See also* Feather Dance
Moon, Goddess of Moon (Coyolxauqui), 83; Links with Virgin Mary, 176; Mythology: Aztec, 39–41; Lacandón, 166; Mythology, 49; Pyramid of the Moon (Teotihuacán), 41, 42
Mosaic, Stone: Mitla, 104 (*105*); Teotihuacán, 42, 43; Uxmal, 154–6 (*154–6*); Turquoise: 44, 106 (*44*, *107*)
Mounds, El Tajín, 46; Olmec, 30, 32; Maya, 123–5; Toltec, 61
Murals, *see* Wall Paintings
Museums in Mexico, 19; Mobile museum (*Casa del Museo*), 23–8 (*24–7*); Museo Nacional de Antropologia e Historia, 23, 25, 28, 84
Music and musicians, 18, 34, 37, 45, 50, 53, 70, 106, 116, 119, 143, 191, 192, 194, 203, 209, 213, 214, 218 (*192*, *210*). *See also* Conch shell trumpets, Drums, Flutes, Guitars, Harps, Rattles and Violins.
Mythology, 22; Aztec, 39–41, 66, 77; Huichol, 201–3, 211, 213, 216, 218; Lacandón, 166–7; Maya (Pre-C) 121–2; Mayo, 177–8; Totonac, 48–9

Nahua Indians, 79–82 (*15*, *80–2*; **7**, **8**, **32**, **33**)
Nahuatl, 23, 65, 73, 79, 80, 111, 215
Najá, 137–42, 166–70; Lake Najá, (*121*, *135*)
Nanauatzin, 39, 41, 49
Napoleon III, 14
Nayarit, 195
Nierika, 217, 218 (*217*; **38**)
Night of the Dead, *see* Day of the Dead
Numerical systems, 11, 23, 120, 124, 127–9, 132, 137 (*129*)
Nunnery (Uxmal), 154, 155 (*153–5*)

Oaxaca City, 92, 109, 110
Oaxaca State, 23, 36, 87–119, 120

Obregón, Alvaro, 14, 172
Observatories, Chichén Itzá, 160; Monte Albán, 90, 91 (*90*); Palenque, 147; Xochicalco, 57, 58
Obsidian, 29, 44, 106, 120
Ocós, 123
Oil, 11, 28
Olmec civilisation, 23, 30–3, 36, 46, 50, 124, 128 (*31–3*; **20**, **22**); Links with Maya civilisation, 122, 124, 127, 128; Spread of Olmec influence: Monte Albán, 89–91; Tlatilco, 36–8
Onyx, 106
Ortega, Father, 195
Otomí Indians, 63–5 (*64*, *65*)

Pacal, Maya Lord, 151
Pacific Ocean, 9, 45, 73, 87, 111, 123, 125, 200
Palaces (*Pre-C*): Aztec: Tenochtitlán, 68; Palace of Montezuma, 69, 70; Maya, 120, 143; Palenque, 147 (*145*; **9**); Uxmal, the Governor's Palace, 155–7; Yaxchilán, 132
Palenque, 145–51, 157, 167, 168 (*145–50*; **9**, **10**)
Palmas, 52 (*52*)
Pariserom, 179, 183–5, 187, 189, 190. *See also* Pharisees and Pilatos
Paskola Dancers, 180, 190–4 (*191*)
Paskome, 179–81, 184, 193, 194
Paz, Octavio, 186
Petén, 123, 125, 129
Petroleos Mexicanos (PEMEX), 11
Peyote, 214–20; Peyote God, 216
Pharisees, 179–90 (*177–89*; **35**)
Pilatos, 179, 181 (*182*; **36**). *See also* Pariserom
Plumed Serpent, *see* Kukulcan and Quetzalcoatl. Pyramid of the Plumed Serpent (Xochicalco), 57 (*57*)
Poetry, 11; Aztec poetry, 70, 84, poems, 79, 85–6; Maya poems, *see* Chilam Balam and Popol Vuh. *See also* Songs
Popol Vuh, 120–2, 129, 167
Popoloca Indians, 88
Population, Pre-C: Teotihuacán, 42; Tenochtitlán, 68.
　Post-C: Bacavachi, 174; Huichol, 195; Lacandón, 136; Maya, 164; Mayo, 171; Mexico: Indian population, 15; Total population, 10; Mexico City, 9, 10; Mixtec, 111; Nahua, 79; Oaxaca State Indian population, 87–8; Otomí, 63; Santo Domingo, 26; Totonac, 47; Zapotec, 92
Portillo, José Lopez, 11, 28
Pottery, Pre-C: 30, 36–8, 44–5, 56, 68, 97–9, 104–5, 123–5, 157, 164–5 (*36–9*, *53*, *97–9*, *105*, *115*, *130*; **22**)
　Post-C: 16, 17, 20, 47, 54, 93, 94, 99, 114, 141
Potting (*Post-C*): Mayo, 175; Mixtec, 114; Tzeltal, 165; Zapotec, 99–102 (*100*, *101*)
Poultry, 10, 49, 81, 92, 94, 95, 99, 112, 137, 167
Prescott, W. H., 41
Priestly caste (indigenous), *Pre-C*: 16, 19, 71, 73, 76, 91, 97, 103, 104, 105, 109, 110, 127, 137, 148, 149, 163, 215; Priesthood as rulers, 42, 46, 70, 127, 151
　Post-C: *See* Shamans and Spiritual leaders
Priests (Catholic), 18, 178; Anticlerical movement, 173, 178; Augustinians, 12; Dominicans, 12; Franciscans, 12, 199, 219; Jesuits, 12, 171, 176, 178; *See also* Missionaries
Projectile points, 120, 123
Proskouriakoff, Tatania, 132, 133

Protestantism, 20, 137
Puebla, 87, 102
Pulque, 60, 64 (*65*)
Puuc, hills, 153; style of architecture, 153–4
Pyramids, 20; Chichén Itzá, Temple-pyramid of Kukulcan, 157–8; Cuicuilco, 38 (*38*); El Tajín, Pyramid of the Niches, 46 (*46*, **1**); La Venta, 32; Maya, 125; Monte Albán, 91, 92, 102 (**15**); Olmec, 31, 32; Santa Cecilia (*85*); Palenque, 148; Temple of the Inscriptions, 147, 150 (*150*); Teotihuacán, Pyramids of the Sun and Moon, 41, 42, 77 (*42*, **16**); Tenayuca, (*84*); Tenochtitlán, 69, 73, 78, 83 (*68*); Tikal, 129 (*126*); Tula, 61, 62 (*62*, *63*); Uxmal, Pyramid of the Magician, 153, 154 (*153*; **11**); Xochicalco, Pyramid of the Plumed Serpent, 57 (*57*)

Quetzal Dance, 81, 82, (*82*; **33**)
Quetzalcoatl (known also as the Feathered or Plumed Serpent), 39, 42, 43, 59–61, 63, 69, 77, 78, 157 (*75*); Pyramid of the Plumed Serpent, Xochicalco, 57 (*57*); Temple of Quetzalcoatl, Teotihuacán, 43 (*43*). *See also* Kulkulcan and Topiltzin.
Quiché Maya, 120, 122
Quintana Roo, 120

Rain, 111; Associations with cross, 18; with Jaguar God, 114; with St Thomas, 18; Huichol rain symbols, 207, 213; Rain petitioners, 81; Rain rituals, 116, 209–10; Rain gods: Huichol, 202, 211, 220. *See also* Chac, Cocijo, Metzabok, Tlaloc
Rattles, gourd, 81, 118, 209, 214 (*193*, *214*); metal and wood, 191
Revolution of 1910, 13, 14, 172
Rituals, *see* Ceremonies
Roman Catholicism, *see* Christianity
Rubber, 31, 51, 167, 170
Rulers (*Pre-C*), 16, 69, 70, 97, 110, 143, 148. *See also* Montezuma, Pacal and Priesthood
Ruz Lhuillier, Alberto, 149, 150, 151

Sacrifice: Animal, 60, 116, 218, 219, (*219*); Human, 52, 53, 55, 59, 60, 61, 63, 73, 76, 86, 103, 109, 151, 157, 160–2; Self-inflicted bleeding, 143
Sahagún, Bernardino de (*La Historia General de las Cosas de la Nueva Espanâ*), 22, 23, 33, 39, 41, 59, 64, 70, 109, 215 (Codex ill. *72*, *109*)
Saints, 18, 33, 49, 81, 119, 166, 176, 178, 201; St Francis, 81; St John, 18; St Martin, 117; St Thomas, 18; Mayo Saints, St Damien and Sta Teresa, 173
San Andrés Cohamiata, 219–20
San Bartolo Coyotepec, 99–101
San Lorenzo, 32, 124
San Martín Tilcajete, 94–6, 117–19
San Luis Potosí, 200, 216
Santa Catarina, 200
Santa Cecilia, 84 (*85*)
Santa Isabel Ixtápan, 29
Santa Marta, 123
Santo Domingo, 26–8
Schools, *see* Education
Sculpture (in stone): *Pre-C*: Aztec, 23, 83, 84, (*23*, *72*, *74*, *75*, *77*, *83*); Dancer slabs at Monte Albán, 89–91 (*89*); El Tajín, 52 (*52*, *53*); Maya, 57, 61, 120, 124, 125, 128, 129, 131 (*124*, *128*, *131*, Codex ill. *125*); Chichén Itzá, 157, 160, 161 (*158*, *159*, *162*); Palenque, 147, 148, 151 (*149–52*); Uxmal, 154–6 (*154–6*); Yaxchilán, 132–3 (*133*; **35**); Olmec, 23, 30–3 (*32*, *33*); Teotihuacán, 43, 44 (*43*); Toltec at Tula, 61–3 (*61–3*); Xochicalco, 56, 57 (*57*)

Post-C: Huichol, 219

Serpents: links with gods, 97, 155, *see also* Quetzalcoatl; Myths, 66, 167; Representations of, 43, 52, 61, 63, 65, 75, 151, 157, 160, 207, 219 (*84, 158*; **13**)

Seventh Day Adventism, 137

Shamans, 19, 20, 37; Huichol (*Mara'akame*), 202–6, 208, 209, 211, 213, 214, 217, 218 (*203, 204, 215*); Lacandón (*T'o'ohil*), 137, 167, 168 (*137, 167, 170*). *See also* Spiritual leaders

Sierra Madre, 9, 171, 195, 197, 205, 216, 220 (*196*)

Silver, 13, 63, 105, 106, 109, 110

Sinaloa, 171, 173

Songs: Huichol Song of Wirikuta, 220; Huichol shamans as singers, 203, 218; Lacandón Jaguar Song, 168; Prayer, 170. *See also* Poems

Sonora, 171, 173, 175

Spain, 12

Spaniards, 11–15, 18, 22, 67, 69, 73, 76, 78, 83, 105, 110, 111, 126, 136–8, 151, 154, 163, 166, 167, 171, 195, 197, 216, 218

Spanish chroniclers, 22, 33, 50–3, 70. *See also* Díaz del Castillo, Landa, Sahagún

Spanish Conquest, 11, 12, 16, 67, 76, 78, 79, 110, 111, 163 (Codex ill. *79*). *See* Feather Dance

Spanish introductions from the Old World, 10, 16, 110, 167, 197, 218

Spiritual leaders, Mayo (*temasti*), 178, 184, 187–90 (*179*). *See* Shamans

Squash, 10, 16, 48, 49, 95, 112, 140, 174, 198, 213, 214

Squatters, 26

Stelae, Maya, 124, 125, 128, 129, 164 (*125, 128, 129, 131, 143*); Monte Albán, 90; Olmec, 32

Stephens, John L., 145, 147, 155–7, 164

Stone tools, 29, 36, 42, 48, 76, 109, 120, 123

Summer Institute of Linguistics, 20, 137

Sun, 33, 50, 72, 148; Aztec cult of the Sun, 73; Era of Fifth Sun, 49; Gods: Aztec, 72; Huichol (Sun Father), 201, 202, 206, 211, 220 (*38*); Lacandón (K'in), 167; Maya, 148; Zapotec, 117; Myths: Aztec, 39–41, 77; Huichol, 201; Lacandón, 166; Totonac, 48, 49; Pyramid of the Sun (Teotihuacán), 41, 42 (*42*; **16**); Sun Stone, 23 (*77*); Temple of the Sun (Palenque), 148. For Solar systems, *see* Calendar Systems

Tabasco, 11, 120, 122

Tamaulipas, 122

Tejada, Lerdo de, 14

Temples: *Pre-C*: Chichén Itzá, Temple of the Jaguars, 160; Temple of the Warriors, 160 (*159*; **12, 13**); Temple-pyramid of Kulculan, 157, 158; Copán, 129; Malinalco, 84; Maya, 120, 123, 125, 142; Mitla, 111 (*112*); Monte Albán, 91, 92, 102; Palenque, 147,

148; Temple of the Cross, 148; Temple of the Foliated Cross, 148 (**10**); Temple of the Inscriptions, 147, 149–51 (*149–51*); Temple of the Sun, 148; Santa Cecilia, 85 (*85*); Tenayuca, 84 (*84*); Tenochtitlán, 68–70, 73, 76, 78, 83 (*68*); Teotihuacán (including Temple of Quetzalcoatl), 42, 43 (*43*); Tula, 61; Uxmal, Temple-pyramid of the Magician, 154 (*153*); Xochicalco, Temple of the Plumed Serpent, 57 (*57*); Yaxchilán, 132, 134; Temple of Hachakyum, 169, 170 (*134*) *Post-C*: Huichol (*calihuey*), 205, 209, 213; Lacandón godhouse, 166, 167, 170 (*167*)

Tenayuca, 84 (*84*)

Tenochtitlán, 67–73, 78, 79, 83 (*68*)

Teotihuacán, 39–46, 55–9, 120, 127, 157 (*40–5*; **16**)

Tepanec, 66

Tepantitla, 44 (*45*)

Textiles, 17, 20, 23, 45, 64, 65, 68, 73, 94, 103, 106, 124, 164, 175, 205–7, 213 (*115*). *See also* Costume

Tezcatlipoca, 55, 59–61, 63, 65, 69, 77

Tezozomoc, 66

Thompson, Eric, 132

Three Marys, 184 (*181, 184*)

Tiger Dance, *see* Jaguar Dance

Tikal, 125, 127, 129, 157 (*126*)

Tin, 110 (*111*)

Tlacolula market, 92–4 (**1**)

Tlaloc, 39, 42, 43, 44, 69, 83

Tlatelolco, 68

Tlatilco, 36–7 (*36, 37*)

Tobacco, 140, 198; Tobacco plantations, 14

Toltec civilization, 23, 59–63, 65–7, 77 (*61–3*; **17**); Influence on Maya, 157, 162, 163 (*158, 159*; **12, 13**)

Tomb Seven at Monte Albán, *see* Burials

Tonantzin, 18

Topiltzin, 59–61, 64. *See* Quetzalcoatl

Tortillas, 15, 16, 93, 95, 112, 114, 140, 202, 211 (*94*)

Totoltepec, 34–6

Totonac *Pre-C*, 46, 50, 52 (*47, 51–3*; **14**); *Post-C*, 46–50, 54 (*19, 48, 49, 55*; **29, 30**)

Trade: *Pre-C*, 45, 46, 71, 73; *Post-C*, 16, 17, 48, 63, 92, 99, 141, 165, 173, 174, 181, 217

Tree of Life, 18, 148, 167

Tres Zapotes, 32

Tribute, 69, 71, 73 (Codex ill. *71*)

Trique Indians, 88 (*87*; **4**)

Tula, 59–63, 64, 65, 157, 160 (*61–3*; **17**)

Turquoise mosaic, 44, 106 (*44, 107*)

Tzeltal Indians, 165–6, 168 (*165, 166*)

Uaxactún, 125, 127, 129

UNESCO, 24

United States of America, 9, 11, 14, 20, 29, 96, 122, 137, 171, 173

Usumacinta River, 131

Uxmal, 153–7 (*153–6*; **11**)

Valley of Mexico, 25, 56, 59, 65, 66

Vazquéz, Mario, 23–8

Velasco family (tinsmiths), 110

Veracruz, 87, 122

Villa, Pancho, 14

Violin or fiddle, 191, 203, 209, 218 (*210*)

Virgin Mary, 18, 177, 194; Links with Moon, 176; Virgin of Jaquila, 117; Virgin of Guadalupe, 12, 13, 117; Virgin of Solitude, 117

Voladores Dance, 49–50 (*49, 50*; **29, 30**)

Wall paintings: Bonampak, 142–5 (*144*); Cacaxla, 21 (*21*; **23**); Chichén Itzá, 157; Mitla, 104; Teotihuacán, 43–5 (*44*); Tepantitla, 44 (*45*)

Warfare: Indigenous battles, 55, 61, 66–7, 71–3, 103–4; Representations of war, 21, 133, 143, 157 (*144*); Wars with Spaniards, 78, 136, 163 (Codex ill. *79*)

Warriors, 45, 55, 61, 63, 65, 66, 71–3, 83, 103, 104, 143, 145 (*21, 34, 62, 72, 76, 130*, Codex ill. *73*), *see* Eagle and Jaguar Knights; Temple of the Warriors (Chichén Itzá), 160 (*159*; **12, 13**). For Gods of War, *see* Huitzilopochtli and Tezcatlipoca

Weaving, 16; Maya, 164–5; Mayo, 175; Mixtec, 114–17 (*114*)

Well (sacred), 161 (*161*)

Were-jaguars, *see* Jaguar

Wheel, 39 (*39*); Zapotec wheel, 100 (*100*)

Wirikuta, 216, 218, 220

Wood carving, 16, 95, 96, (*97*)

Writing systems, 11, 21, 31, 45, 77, 89–91, 124, 127, 132–3, 137. *See also* Codices and Hieroglyphs

Wycliffe Bible Translators, 20

Xipe Totec (The Flayed One), 97, 98, 109 (*77, 98*; **18**)

Xitli, 38

Xochicalco, 56–9 (*56–8*)

Xochipilli, (*23*)

Yaqui Indians, 171

Yarn paintings, *see* nierikas

Yaxchilán, 131–4, 167, 169–70 (*133, 134, 170*; **21**)

Yokes, 52 (*52*)

Yucatán peninsula, 9, 61, 120, 151, 153, 157, 162, 163

Yucatec Maya, 123, 136, 151, 154, 157, 161

Zaachila, 104, 105

Zacatecas, 195

Zapata, Emiliano, 14

Zapotec civilisation: *Pre-C*: 23, 88, 91–2, 97–9, 102, 104–5, 109 (*92, 97–9*; **15**); *Post-C*: 13, 88, 92–6, 99–102, 117–19, 171 (*94, 97, 100, 101, 118, 119*; **1, 34**)

Zapotec wheel, 100 (*100*)

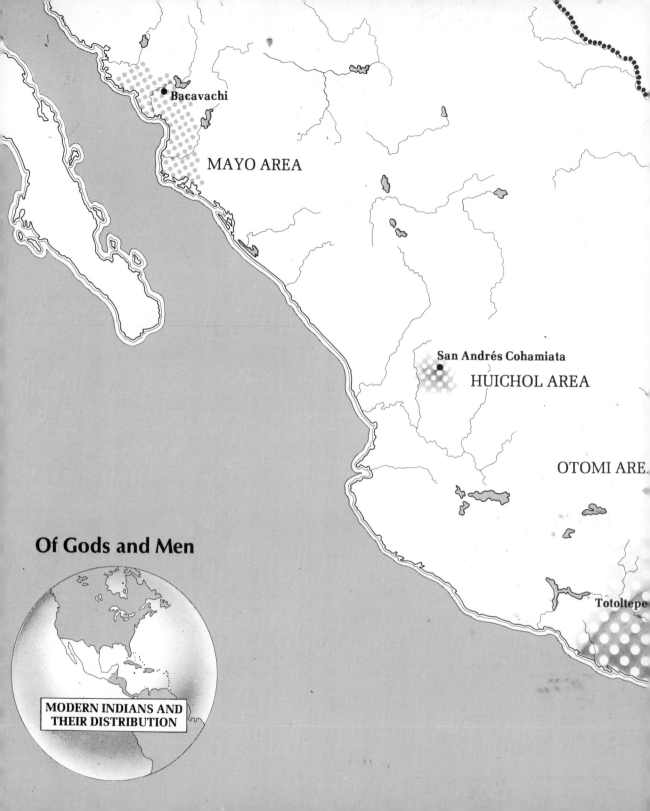

Bacavachi

MAYO AREA

San Andrés Cohamiata

HUICHOL AREA

OTOMI ARE

Of Gods and Men

MODERN INDIANS AND
THEIR DISTRIBUTION

Totoltepe